SMP 16–19

Mechanics 1

Motion and force

CAMBRIDGE
UNIVERSITY PRESS

Much of this book is based on earlier SMP books to which the following people contributed.

Chris Belsom	Paul Roder
Stan Dolan	Tom Roper
Judith Galsworthy	Mike Savage
Andy Hall	Bernard Taylor
Mike Hall	Carole Tyler
Janet Jagger	Nigel Webb
Ann Kitchen	Julian Williams
Melissa Rodd	Phil Wood

PUBLISHED BY THE PRESS SYNDICATE OF THE UNIVERSITY OF CAMBRIDGE
The Pitt Building, Trumpington Street, Cambridge, United Kingdom

CAMBRIDGE UNIVERSITY PRESS
The Edinburgh Building, Cambridge, CB2 2RU, UK
40 West 20th Street, New York, NY 10011–4211, USA
10 Stamford Road, Oakleigh, VIC 3166, Australia
Ruiz de Alarcón 13, 28014 Madrid, Spain
Dock House, The Waterfront, Cape Town 8001, South Africa

http://www.cambridge.org

First published 2001

Printed in the United Kingdom at the University Press, Cambridge

Typeface Minion and Officina   *System* QuarkXpress®

A catalogue record for this book is available from the British Library

ISBN 0 521 78800 5 paperback

Acknowledgements

The authors and publishers would like to thank the following for supplying photographs:

page   v   Ann Ronan Picture Library
page   53   The Stock Market Photo Agency Inc. (golfer); PhotoDisc (discus thrower); PhotoDisc (airplane)
Page   64   The Stock Market Photo Agency Inc.
page 103   Mechanics in Action/Ann Kitchen
page 104   Mechanics in Action/Ann Kitchen

We have been unable to trace the copyright holder of the photograph on page 9, and would be grateful for
any information that would enable us to do so.

The map on page 28 is reproduced on behalf of Ordnance Survey® on behalf of The Controller of Her
Majesty's Stationery Office. © Crown Copyright 2000. Licence no. 399671.

Cover photograph: Bernhard Edmaier/Science Photo Library

Contents

Sir Isaac Newton 1642–1727

Using this book

Most sections within a chapter consist of work developing new ideas followed by an exercise for practice in using those ideas.

Within the development sections, some questions and activities are labelled with a **D**, for example **2D**, and are enclosed in a box. These involve issues that are worth exploring through discussion – either teacher-led discussion in the whole class or discussion by students in small groups, who may then feed back their conclusions to the whole class.

Questions labelled **E** are more demanding.

1 Modelling motion

A Introduction (answers p. 125)

The foundations of modern mechanics were laid by Sir Isaac Newton (1642–1727) at the University of Cambridge. He published his **law of universal gravitation** in 1667 and his three **laws of motion** in the *Principia* in 1687.

A study of Newtonian mechanics will give insight into many of the natural phenomena of the world. For example, the tides, the equatorial bulge of the Earth, the time periods of the planets, the paths of comets and the variation in gravity at different latitudes were all explained by Sir Isaac Newton.

Applications of Newtonian mechanics are still extremely important today, especially in engineering, science and technology. For instance, using just A level mechanics, it is possible to

- design road humps suitable for enforcing a 30 m.p.h. speed limit
- estimate the best rotational speed for a tumble drier
- choose a suitable counterweight for the design of a roadblock for a customs post or car park
- calculate the height and speed of a geostationary communications satellite.

Your study of mechanics will help you to 'explain and predict' a range of events and phenomena in the physical world. This section will introduce you to the types of event in which we are interested, i.e. to which mechanics can contribute an important new insight.

Simple experiments

1D | Many simple everyday events have results you might not expect. For each of the situations below, describe what you would expect to observe. Check what happens in practice.

(a) A cricket ball and a golf ball are dropped together. Which will hit the ground first?

(b) A full can of cola and an empty one roll downhill. Which can takes the shorter time to roll down the slope?

(c) A friend holds a bicycle upright.
What happens if you push backwards on the lower pedal?

(d) What happens when you stand on a set of bathroom scales and press down with a broom (i) on the scales, (ii) on the floor?

The situations in (a) and (b) are similar to the classic experiments conducted by Galileo Galilei (1564–1642). He was concerned primarily with describing the trajectory of cannon balls.

Galileo was an Italian scientist and astronomer whose work at the University of Padua preceded that of Newton. His investigations into the motion of falling and rolling bodies included a study of the motion of spheres down inclined planes. Using planes of about 2 m in length and fixed at angles of between 1.5° and 2°, Galileo discovered a relationship between the distance travelled from rest and the time taken.

2D   Set up and conduct an experiment similar to Galileo's.

What precautions should you take to make your results consistent?

How can you ensure the accuracy of your results?

What is the relationship between distance and time?

Write down your observations. You will need them later.

B Applied mathematical modelling (answers p. 126)

As you progress with your study of mechanics you will be able to make predictions based upon Newton's laws. You will then be able to use observations and measurements to compare your predictions with reality.

The stages in problem solving are summarised in the following diagram.

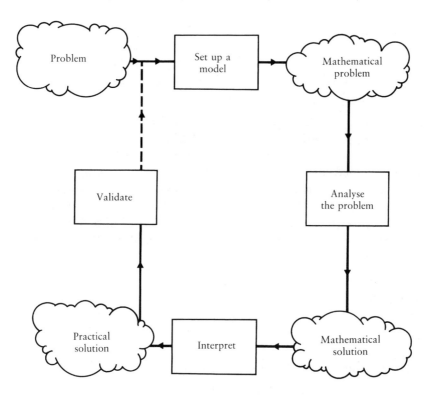

The actions you are expected to carry out during the problem-solving process are

- identification of interesting **problems** to solve
- formulation of the problem in mathematical terms, which involves **setting up a model**
- **analysis of the problem** to obtain a mathematical solution
- **interpretation** of the solution in real terms, and **validation** of it through your observations or experience.

In restaging Galileo's experiments in Section A, the actions you should have performed can be summarised as follows.

This stage requires the identification of a problem to be solved, such as

- to find the distance the ball will roll down the slope in any given time
- to find the time the ball will take to roll any given distance.

Other problems include finding the speed of the ball, or its acceleration.

Set up a model

Now you collect data on distance and time. You may choose variables to represent distance and time, d and t. The mathematical problem then is to find a relationship between d and t.

Analyse the problem

You should then analyse your data by drawing a graph and by trying to express d as a function of t, $d(t)$. A function graph plotter or a graphic calculator can be used to find a particular function such as $d = kt$ or $d = kt^2$ which best fits the data and provides a mathematical solution to the problem. Further analysis might give a formula for the speed or acceleration of the ball.

Interpret

You should now interpret your solution in ordinary English language, for example

- the ball will roll 1 metre in 2.85 seconds
- the ball will roll 0.38 m in 1 second
- the ball is gaining speed
- the average speed of the ball in the first second is ...

and so on.

Validate

These interpretations can now usually be validated in practice! You should check your predictions experimentally and confirm that your mathematical model is valid. If it is *not* valid, you may need to return to the first stage and reconsider your model.

This is an example of mathematical modelling. The function $d(t)$ is a mathematical model of the motion of the rolling ball, and can be used to make quantitative predictions about its real motion. Other examples of modelling will be seen throughout this chapter.

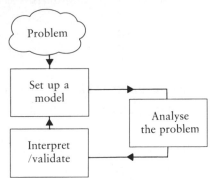

There is an alternative approach, often pursued by engineers and scientists, at the stage of setting up a model. By thinking theoretically about the factors involved in the situation and making simplifying assumptions, they can suggest a formula or equation likely to act as a suitable mathematical model. Observations can be made, the model tested and, all being well, validated.

In 1687, Sir Isaac Newton published a remarkably simple framework for a model of motion which is as relevant today as it was in the seventeenth century. As you work through this chapter you will gain an understanding of the three 'laws' of motion which formed the basis of Newton's model.

Experiments

Three experiments are described below. You should do *at least one* of these before discussing all the experiments with your teacher and fellow students. At this stage, there is no need to try to explain the results. You should simply attempt an analysis of your measurements to enable you to make predictions which can be tested experimentally.

You will find it helpful to use a modelling diagram for this analysis.

1 *The bricklayer's lament*
   (based on a story by Gerard Hoffnung)

Respected Sir

When I got to the top of the building I found that a lot of bricks were missing so I rigged up a beam and a pulley and hoisted up a couple of barrels of bricks. When I had finished there were a lot of bricks left over so I hoisted the barrel to the top again and secured the line at the bottom. I then filled the barrel with bricks and climbed down. I cast off the line but unfortunately the barrel of bricks was heavier than I was and before I knew what was happening the barrel started down jerking me off my feet. I decided to hang on. Halfway up I met the barrel coming down and received a severe blow to my shoulder. I continued up and hit my head on the beam. When the barrel reached the bottom, the bricks spilled out. I was now heavier than the barrel and started coming down again at high speed. Halfway down I met the barrel coming up and got another severe blow. When I hit the ground I must have lost my presence of mind for I let go of the line. The barrel then came down again hitting me on the head and putting me in hospital.

I respectfully request sick leave.

Find a model for the motion of the bricklayer and the barrel.

Hints

Set up the apparatus shown.

(a) Find the time taken for the 100-gram mass to hit the floor when it is released 60 cm above the floor.

(b) How long does it take when it is released 70 cm above the floor?

(c) Repeat for other distances.

(d) Make a table or a graph.

(e) Find a general rule and test it.

(f) Where can you go from here?

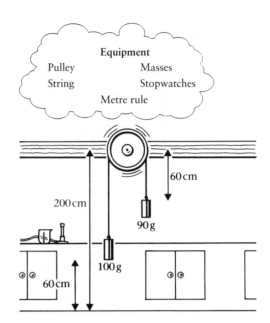

2   Find a model for the motion of a rolling ball.

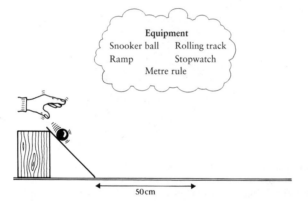

Hints

(a) How long will the ball take to roll 50 cm along the track? How long will it take to roll 75 cm?

(b) Estimate how far it will travel in 1 second.

(c) Take careful measurements for several different distances.

(d) Plot a graph of distance against time. Find a general rule for the motion and test it.

(e) What happens if the ball rolls along a carpet or cloth? Repeat your experiment with a strip of ribbon or felt in the track. Remember to record your results carefully.

3 Find a model for the motion of a ball rolling across a sloping plane.

Equipment
Sugar paper   Water
Wooden blocks
Tape measure
Stopwatch   Ramp
Snooker ball or smooth
  hard rubber ball

Hints

(a) Roll the ball gently down the ramp so that it rolls onto the table.

(b) Adjust the height of release so that the ball traces a curve similar to that in the diagram.

(c) Now dampen the ball and release it from the same point on the ramp. Go over the path of the ball with a felt-tip pen.

(d) Using the same release point each time, find how long it takes for the ball to reach A, B, C and D. (A ruler placed as a stop will help you to time accurately.)

(e) Cut around the path and stick it onto squared paper. Mark your times on the graph.

(f) Find and test a general rule.

After working through this chapter you should

1   have some appreciation of what is meant by a mathematical model and how you may arrive at one and test it

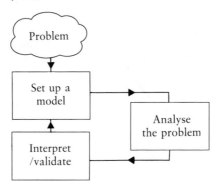

2   understand how mathematical modelling enables you to predict the motion of objects

3   be aware that there is much you do not understand about the behaviour of things in motion!

2 Kinematics

A Motion (answers p. 127)

In this chapter you will not be trying to find out what causes
something to start or stop moving. Rather, you will be investigating
what the motion is like.

This branch of mathematics is called **kinematics**, the study of
movement.

To help describe a real-life example of motion, you can often set up a
mathematical model of the actual motion. Various simplifying
assumptions are made so that you can study the motion without
having to consider all the factors which inevitably complicate matters
in the real example.

You might, for example, ignore the size of an object and consider it to
be a **particle** – an object whose mass is concentrated at a single point;
or you might consider the motion to take place in a precise straight
line, ignoring any small deviations from such a path. Whenever you set
up such a model, you should be clear about the assumptions you are
making.

For the time being, you will assume that you can model the motions
studied by considering the motion of a particle.

1D	What are the three physical quantities measured by the instruments pictured above?
	What aspects of a car's motion are **not** represented by these quantities?

B Average speed (answers p. 127)

One important question which can be asked about any moving object is 'What is its speed?'

In the Système Internationale (SI), the basic units of length and time are metres (m) and seconds (s). The basic unit of speed is therefore metres per second (m s^{-1}).

On a particular straight road, lamp-posts are spaced every 180 metres. A girl takes 60 seconds to run between one pair of lamp-posts and 90 seconds to walk between the next pair. She continues along the road alternately running and walking.

When running, the average speed is

$$\frac{180}{60} = 3 \text{ m s}^{-1}.$$

When walking, the average speed is

$$\frac{180}{90} = 2 \text{ m s}^{-1}.$$

1D Why is the overall average speed not simply $\dfrac{3 + 2}{2} = 2.5 \text{ m s}^{-1}$?

$$\text{Average speed} = \frac{\text{Distance covered}}{\text{Time taken}}$$

Example 1

Scouts' pace consists of alternately running and walking an equal number of steps; for example, 40 running, 40 walking, 40 running, and so on. This enables large distances to be covered easily.

Problem

How long would it take a Scout to cover 2 km?

What is the average speed of the Scout?

Solution

> Set up a model

Assumptions are made to simplify the problem; if any of these are poor assumptions you can modify them later.

● Assume the Scout's steps are all the same length, 1 metre.
● Assume the Scout runs at a steady rate of 3 m s^{-1} and walks at a steady 2 m s^{-1}.

> Analyse the problem

The distance travelled in 40 steps is 40 metres, whether the Scout walks or runs.

The time taken to run 40 steps at 3 m s^{-1} is $\dfrac{40}{3} = 13.3$ seconds.

The time taken to walk 40 steps at 2 m s^{-1} is $\dfrac{40}{2} = 20$ seconds.

The (time, distance) graph shows the motion of the Scout.

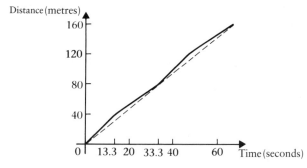

The average speed over 80 m is $\dfrac{80}{33.3}$ or 2.4 m s^{-1}.

The time taken to cover 2 km or 2000 m is approximately $\dfrac{2000}{2.4}$ or 833 seconds.

> Interpret

Both the main assumptions might be wrong in practice, so the answer should be rounded and regarded only as an approximation. Our conclusion that a Scout takes about 14 minutes to travel 2 km could be validated by suitable experiments.

Notice that the average speed is less than the mean of the two speeds. This is because the Scout spends more *time* walking than running.

Exercise B (answers p. 127)

1   Find the average speed of a jogger who runs for 30 seconds at 5 m s^{-1} and then walks at 2 m s^{-1} for an equal period of time.

2   A jogger runs for 30 seconds at 5 m s^{-1} and then walks an equal distance at 2 m s^{-1}. What is her average speed?

3   A girl runs for 60 m at 3 m s^{-1} and then walks twice as far at a speed of 2 m s^{-1}. What is her average speed?

4   My average speed on a car journey of 210 miles (338 km) was 42 miles per hour (18.8 m s^{-1}). If my average speed for the first half of the journey's distance was 30 miles per hour (13.4 m s^{-1}), what was my average speed for the second half of the journey?

5E Repeat question 1 for a jogger who runs at $u \text{ m s}^{-1}$ and walks at $v \text{ m s}^{-1}$.

6E Repeat question 2 for a jogger who runs at $u \text{ m s}^{-1}$ and walks at $v \text{ m s}^{-1}$.

C   (Time, distance) and (time, speed) graphs (answers p. 128)

In an athletics match, the winner of the 100-metre sprint in the under-13 section took 16.8 seconds and the winner of the 100-metre sprint in the under-18 section took 13.2 seconds. This information could be represented on graphs of distance against time. We shall use the symbols s and t to denote distance and time respectively. These graphs are then called (t, s) graphs.

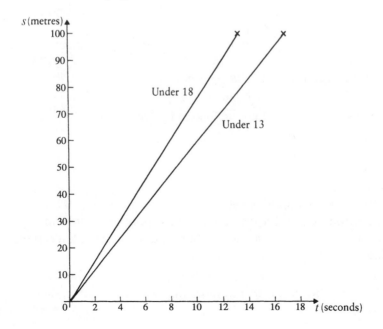

1D What is represented by the gradient, $\dfrac{ds}{dt}$, of each of the lines above?

What information do the corresponding $\left(t, \dfrac{ds}{dt}\right)$ graphs convey about the athletes' motion?

How realistic is this model? How could you improve your model of the motion of the runners?

For the girl on p. 10 who alternately runs and walks between lamp-posts which are 180 metres apart, the $\left(t, \dfrac{ds}{dt}\right)$ graph is as shown here.

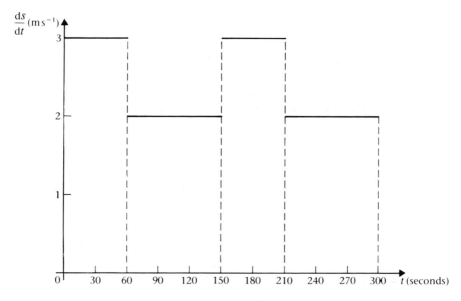

At 3 m s^{-1}, it takes 60 s to run the 180 m between the lampposts. The distance travelled (180 m) is represented by the area underneath the $\left(t, \dfrac{ds}{dt}\right)$ graph. Check that the area of each block gives a distance of 180 m.

The gradient, $\dfrac{ds}{dt}$, of a (t, s) graph gives the speed of the particle at time t.

The area under a $\left(t, \dfrac{ds}{dt}\right)$ graph represents the distance travelled.

2 A simplified (time, distance) graph of a college lecturer's (short) walk
to work one morning is given below.

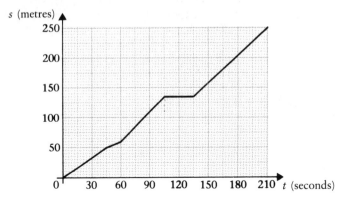

(a) Explain the shape of the (t, s) graph by writing a brief account of
what might have happened.

(b) Draw a $\left(t, \dfrac{ds}{dt}\right)$ graph and check that the information it contains is

consistent with your answer to part (a).

(c) How is the total distance of the journey represented on the (t, s)

graph and on the $\left(t, \dfrac{ds}{dt}\right)$ graph?

(d) What was happening 2 minutes after the lecturer left home? How
is this represented on each graph?

(e) When did the lecturer travel most quickly? How is this
represented on each graph?

The graph of distance against time for a journey made up of several
sections, each taken at constant speed, is continuous and consists of
jointed straight line segments.

Considering the $\left(t, \dfrac{ds}{dt}\right)$ and (t, s) graphs, you can see that

Distances covered are represented by changes in height on the
(t, s) graph and by areas underneath the $\left(t, \dfrac{ds}{dt}\right)$ graph.

Speed is represented by gradient on the (t, s) graph and by height
on the $\left(t, \dfrac{ds}{dt}\right)$ graph.

Exercise C (answers p. 128)

1 For part of her pre-race warm up, an athlete jogged at 2.5 m s^{-1} for 15 minutes. Represent this on a graph of speed against time. What distance did she cover? On the graph, how would you represent her coming to a standstill?

2 An athlete's training schedule consists of 20 repetitions of fast running for 1 minute followed by $1\frac{1}{2}$ minutes jog recovery. If his fast running speed is a steady 4.8 m s^{-1} and his jogging speed is 3 m s^{-1}, what distance will he cover in this session?

3 Draw a graph of speed against time for the first 150 seconds of the athlete's motion in question 2. Superimpose the graph of speed against time for someone who moves with the athlete's average speed for the full 150 seconds.

4 (a) This (t, s) graph models the motion of two runners. Draw rough sketches of the corresponding $\left(t, \dfrac{\mathrm{d}s}{\mathrm{d}t}\right)$ graphs and compare briefly how the runners performed during the race.

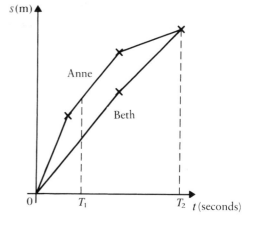

(b) What do you notice about the runners at time T_1? Explain how this is represented in each graph.

(c) Repeat (b) for time T_2.

5 A lorry travelling at an average speed of 11.4 m s^{-1} took $1\frac{1}{2}$ hours to reach the motorway. It then travelled at an average speed of 16.2 m s^{-1} for 2 hours before leaving the motorway and finishing the journey at an average speed of 10.7 m s^{-1} for 45 minutes. How far did the lorry travel?

6 A team of boys challenged a team of girls to see who could cover the greatest distance in 1 hour of Scouts' pace. The boys decided to run at 3 m s^{-1} for 90 seconds and to walk at 2 m s^{-1} for 135 seconds. The girls decided to run at 3 m s^{-1} for 50 seconds and to walk at 2 m s^{-1} for 75 seconds. Draw their respective graphs of speed against time for the first 6 minutes of the race. Assuming that both teams managed to keep up these paces for the full hour, which team won and by how much?

D   Speed (answers p. 129)

Section C considered situations where the speed was constant and the (time, speed) graph consisted of horizontal straight lines. It was clear that in such cases the gradient of the (t, s) graph gave the speed and the area under the $\left(t, \dfrac{ds}{dt}\right)$ graph gave distance. You now need to consider cases where the speed is not necessarily constant, but may change with time. You saw this in the Galileo experiments of Chapter 1 Section A, where the (t, s) graph did not consist of line segments but was a smooth curve. This problem is considered below.

1 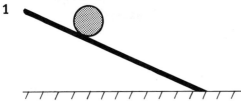 The graph shown below is drawn from data collected by students, from Galileo's experiment. Substitute your own data here if available and draw your own graph.

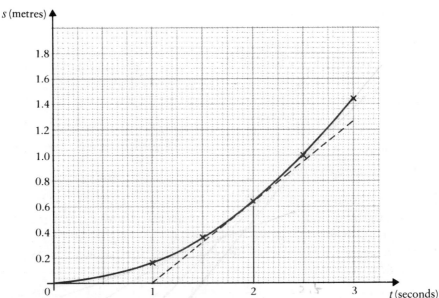

The tangent to the curve at the point where $t = 2$ is shown by the dashed line.

(a)   What is $\dfrac{ds}{dt}$ at $t = 2$? Describe in words what this represents and state the units in which $\dfrac{ds}{dt}$ is measured.

(b) Find the gradient of the curve at half-second intervals.

(c) Plot the corresponding $\left(t, \dfrac{ds}{dt}\right)$ graph. Describe in words what you note about the graph and what it implies about the motion of the ball.

The gradient of a curved (t, s) graph still represents speed, but this speed is changing. Speed (as opposed to average speed) is always understood to mean instantaneous speed, so that a speed of, say, 10 m s^{-1} means that the object would travel 10 metres every second if it maintained the speed at that instant.

> On a (t, s) graph, this imaginary motion with constant speed is represented by the tangent to the curve.

You may have obtained graphs similar to those below for the motion studied in question 1.

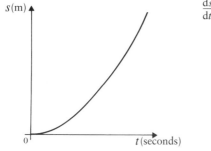
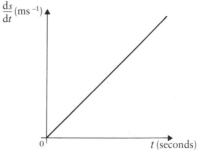

You saw earlier that if the speed is constant, then the area under the graph of speed against time gives the distance travelled. Other examples where the $\left(t, \dfrac{ds}{dt}\right)$ graph is a straight line appear to support this theory. It can be proved that this is true for any graph of speed against time.

> The area under a general $\left(t, \dfrac{ds}{dt}\right)$ graph represents the distance travelled.

Example 2

Describe the motion
represented in this

$\left(t, \dfrac{ds}{dt}\right)$ graph.

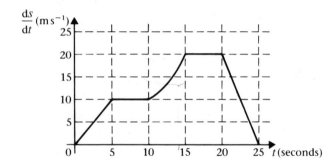

Solution

$t = 0$ to 5 There is a steady increase in speed. The distance covered
each second therefore increases at a constant rate. The
distance covered in the first five seconds is 25 m.

$t = 5$ to 10 Speed remains constant at $10\ \text{m s}^{-1}$. The distance covered
each second is constant. A further 50 m is travelled.

$t = 10$ to 15 Speed increases throughout. The distance covered each
second increases.

(and so on)

Exercise D (answers p. 129)

1 For the motion described in Example 2 above, estimate the distance
travelled:

   (a) between $t = 10$ and $t = 15$ (b) between $t = 20$ and $t = 25$.

2 The $\left(t, \dfrac{ds}{dt}\right)$ graph for a short jog is shown below.

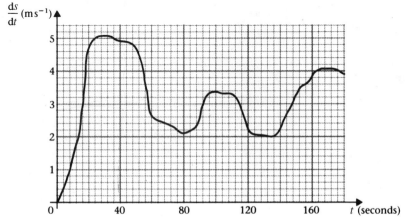

From this (time, speed) graph, estimate the distance travelled in:

(a) 40 seconds   (b) 2 minutes.

3

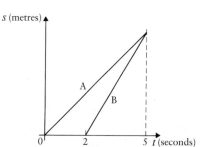

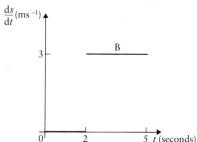

The graphs give some details of the motion of both A and B. At what distance from the start do A and B meet? What is the speed of A?

4 Tracy cycles from Aycliffe to Beford, a distance of 3 miles, in 16 minutes. She rests for 10 minutes before continuing to Ceville, a further distance of 4 miles, which takes 20 minutes.

Simon walks the same journey, does not stop to rest and takes 2 hours.

(a) If Tracy starts out 50 minutes after Simon, where will she overtake him?

(b) What is Tracy's average speed?

(c) What is Simon's average speed?

5 (a) Copy and complete the following graphs of distance against time and speed against time for the first 5 seconds of an object's motion.

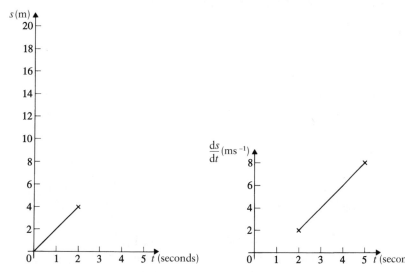

(b) What is the distance covered by the object during this motion?

6

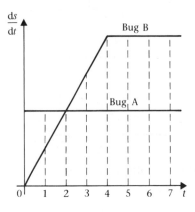

The graphs of speed against time for two gutter-bugs, starting from the same point and crawling along the same gutter, are shown.

(a) Describe the progress of bug A.

(b) Describe the progress of bug B.

(c) When is bug A moving at the same speed as bug B?

(d) When does bug B catch up with bug A?

E Investigations involving speed (answers p. 130)

1D

The Highway Code states:

On an open road, in good conditions, a two-second gap between cars should be sufficient.

What is meant by a two-second gap?

Example 3

In many tunnels there is both a maximum and a minimum speed limit to ensure a good flow of cars through the tunnel.

Problem

The tunnel authorities want to get as many cars through the tunnel as they can in an hour. The safe gap between cars depends on their speed. Suggest sensible speed limits for the tunnel.

Solution

Set up a model

Suppose the cars are 4 metres long and their speed is v m s^{-1}. There must be a two-second gap between each pair of cars. Let the number of cars entering the tunnel each minute be N. You need to maximise N.

Analyse the problem

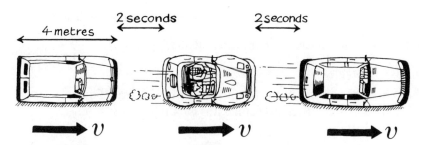

2 seconds   2 seconds
4 metres

The time between the back of one car and the front of the next car passing a certain point is 2 seconds.

The time taken for one car to pass is $\frac{4}{v}$ seconds. So the total time between successive cars entering the tunnel is

$$2 + \frac{4}{v} \text{ seconds} = \frac{2v+4}{v} \text{ seconds}.$$

The number of cars a minute entering the tunnel is

$$N = 60 \div \frac{2v+4}{v} = \frac{60v}{2v+4}.$$

This is easiest to interpret from a graph.

$v \, (\text{m s}^{-1})$	N
1	10
5	21
10	25
15	26
20	27
30	28

Interpret

You can see that the maximum number of cars a minute seems to be 30 when their speed is infinite. A speed of 30 m s^{-1} will enable 28 cars a minute to enter the tunnel. However, the number is about the same for any speed above 10 m s^{-1} (36 km h^{-1}). Below 10 m s^{-1} there is a significant drop in traffic flow. A lower speed limit of 15 m s^{-1} seems sensible, giving $N = 26$. Safety considerations should govern the upper speed limit; it makes little difference to traffic flow.

Validate

For a stream of lorries 10 metres long, a speed of 15 m s^{-1} will allow up to 22 vehicles to pass each minute, calculating from $N = \dfrac{60v}{2v + 10}$.

This is acceptable.

The actual speed range in the Mont Blanc tunnel is from 50 km h^{-1} to 80 km h^{-1}. In the St Bernard tunnel it is 60 km h^{-1} to 80 km h^{-1}.

2

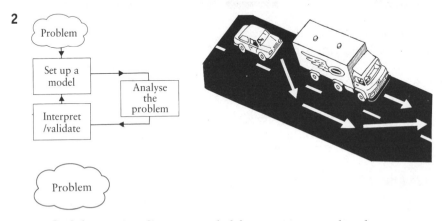

To find the passing distance needed for a car to overtake a lorry moving at a steady speed.

Consider what factors are relevant:

- the performance of the car
- the initial speed of the car
- the speed of the lorry
- the length of the lorry
- the safe distance between vehicles (the two-second rule states that the gap should be at least the distance travelled by the following vehicle in two seconds).

Make assumptions that will simplify the problem. For example, assume that the car is travelling with constant speed as it approaches and passes the lorry.

It might help first to make estimates of any relevant quantities and then to introduce variables.

After working through this chapter you should

1   be aware that simplifying assumptions are necessary so that motion can be modelled mathematically, and be able to discuss how appropriate these assumptions are in simple cases

2   be familiar with the concepts of distance (s metres), speed $\left(\dfrac{\mathrm{d}s}{\mathrm{d}t}\,\mathrm{m\,s^{-1}}\right)$ and time (t seconds)

3   know that the average speed of an object is the constant speed with which it would have covered the same total distance in the same total time, i.e.

$$\text{Average speed} = \frac{\text{Distance covered}}{\text{Time taken}}$$

4   know that speed is the gradient of a (t, s) graph of distance against time

5   know that the total distance travelled is the area underneath a $\left(t, \dfrac{\mathrm{d}s}{\mathrm{d}t}\right)$ graph of speed against time.

3 Vectors

A Introduction (answers p. 131)

When both the direction and the size of a quantity are given, then you are dealing with a **vector** quantity.

Displacement is the word used to describe a distance moved in a certain direction and is an example of a vector.

A quantity which has magnitude or size but not direction is called a **scalar**.

1D | Write down some examples of scalar quantities.

Can you think of any vector quantities other than displacement?

> A scalar quantity has magnitude only.
>
> A vector quantity has magnitude and direction.

A displacement involves two pieces of information – the distance between two points and the direction of one point from the other. For example, a ship sails 10 km on a bearing of 037° (compass bearings are angles measured clockwise from north).

This vector can be represented by the line $\overrightarrow{AB}$ drawn to scale [1 cm : 2 km].

$\overrightarrow{AB}$ is the displacement vector representing the ship's voyage. The arrow over the letters denotes that the direction of the vector is from the first point A to the second point B.

Another way of going from A to B would be to sail 6 km due east to point C and then 8 km due north to B.

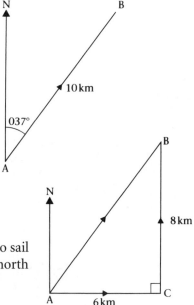

This journey has been drawn to scale [1 cm : 2 km]. You can confirm by measurement or calculation that the distance AB is 10 km, as before, and the bearing of B from A is 037°.

Thinking in terms of the rectangular coordinates of a graph, it can be said that going from A to B involves the ship moving 6 km in the x-direction and 8 km in the y-direction. The 6 and the 8 are called the x- and y-**components** of the vector.

A convention for writing down a vector in terms of its x- and y-components is to use the form $\begin{bmatrix} x \\ y \end{bmatrix}$. This is called a **column vector**.

Thus the vector $\overrightarrow{AB}$ can be expressed in two ways:

$$\overrightarrow{AB} = \begin{bmatrix} 6 \\ 8 \end{bmatrix}$$

or $\overrightarrow{AB} = 10$ km bearing 037°

These are two ways of saying the same thing and it is easy to convert from one to the other.

Example 1

Sketch the vector $\begin{bmatrix} 3 \\ 5 \end{bmatrix}$ and convert it to the distance and bearing form.

Solution

Start by drawing a right-angled triangle.

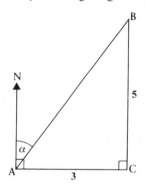

$AB^2 = 3^2 + 5^2 \implies AB = 5.83$ km

$\tan \alpha = \frac{3}{5} \implies \alpha = 31.0° \implies$ bearing 031°

> The distance from A to B is called the **magnitude** of the vector $\overrightarrow{AB}$ and is written as either $|\overrightarrow{AB}|$ or AB.

Example 2

Sketch the displacement vector, 10 km on a bearing 323°, and convert it to a column vector.

Solution

Sketch the vector. Now draw a right-angled triangle.

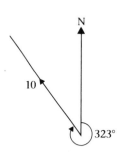
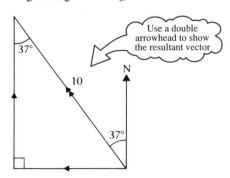

West component = 10 sin 37° = 6.02 ≈ 6 km

North component = 10 cos 37° = 7.99 ≈ 8 km

The column vector is $\begin{bmatrix} -6 \\ 8 \end{bmatrix}$.

Example 3

A motor boat travelling at 35 km h^{-1} on a bearing of 020° is 7.5 km west of a long reef which runs north–south. When will it cross the reef?

Solution

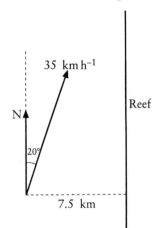

The easterly component of the boat's velocity is 35 sin 20° km h^{-1}. At this easterly velocity it will cover the 7.5 km in

$$\frac{7.5}{35 \sin 20°} = 0.6265 \text{ hour}$$

$$= 38 \text{ minutes}$$

Exercise A (answers p. 131)

1 Sketch the following vectors and convert them into column vector form.
   Check your answers with scale drawings.
   (a) $\overrightarrow{PQ} = 7$ km bearing 060°   (b) $\overrightarrow{RS} = 12$ km bearing 200°
   (c) $\overrightarrow{TU} = 5.2$ km bearing 310°

2 Sketch the following vectors and convert them into distance and bearing form.
   All units are kilometres.

   (a) $\overrightarrow{AB} = \begin{bmatrix} 5 \\ 12 \end{bmatrix}$ (b) $\overrightarrow{CD} = \begin{bmatrix} 16 \\ 16 \end{bmatrix}$ (c) $\overrightarrow{EF} = \begin{bmatrix} -5.5 \\ -8.5 \end{bmatrix}$ (d) $\overrightarrow{GH} = \begin{bmatrix} 3 \\ -4 \end{bmatrix}$

3 A sailor in a catamaran starts from Seaview and sails 440 m on a bearing 064°. He then tacks (changes direction), and sails 580 m on a bearing 129°. Calculate how far east and how far south he is then from Seaview. On what bearing must he sail in order to return there? What assumption have you made when answering this question?

4 A snooker ball travels 22 cm in a direction making an angle of 33° with the x-axis. It then hits a cushion lying parallel to the x-axis, undergoing a 'perfect' rebound, so that its new direction makes −33° with the x-axis. It comes to rest after travelling a further 44 cm. Calculate how far it is then from the starting point and in what direction.

B Vectors and maps (answers p. 132)

Ordnance Survey maps cover the whole of the UK. Each map is divided by grid lines into many squares, the distance between two adjacent lines representing one kilometre on the land. Each grid line is numbered, increasing a kilometre at a time. Places are identified by giving the number of the left-hand and lower boundaries of the square that they are in, just as points on a graph are located by x- and y-coordinates. For example, on the map shown on the next page, the middle of Black Head is at the intersection of the two grid lines numbered 04 and 48. It is possible to estimate a position to 0.1 of a square, or 0.1 km, and so the coordinates of Black Head can be given with greater precision as 04.0 and 48.0.

Similarly, the coordinates of Penare Point are 02.2 and 45.8.

As with graphs, the x-coordinate (or 'easting') is given first, followed by the y-coordinate (or 'northing').

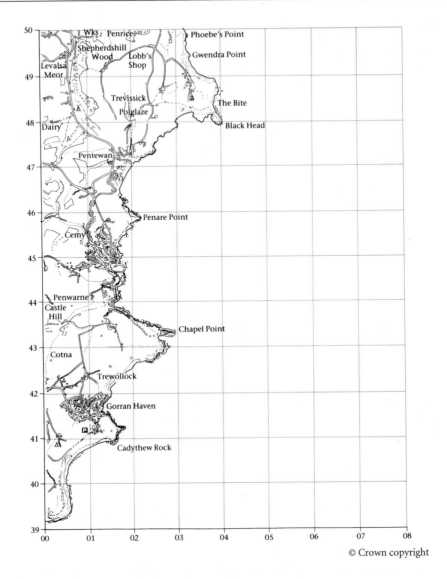

Whenever a map reference of a place is given, the six figures are written down without the decimal points. Thus,

Black Head is at 040480,   Penare Point is at 022458.

It should now be clear that a six-figure map reference contains information about distances, and moreover to an accuracy of 100 metres! Such a map reference can easily be 'dismantled' and turned back into distance coordinates – just cut it in half and insert decimal points! For example,

$$022 \quad \} \quad 458$$
$$\downarrow \qquad \quad \downarrow$$
$$2.2 \quad \} \quad 45.8$$

1D

Confirm your understanding of six-figure map references.

(a) Write down the references of Phoebe's Point and Cadythew Rock.

(b) State what can be found at 002480 and at 038483.

(c) Change 024473 and 032505 into distance coordinates.

Starting with just the map references of two places it is easy to calculate the shortest distance between them and the direction of one from the other, using what you have learnt about vectors.

Example 4

Calculate the bearing of Black Head (040480) from Penare Point (022458) and the shortest distance between them.

Solution

Start by 'dismantling' the map references, i.e. express them as coordinates.

	x	y
Black Head (B)	4.0	48.0
Penare Point (P)	2.2	45.8
Differences	1.8	2.2

Thus B is 1.8 km east and 2.2 km north of P. Expressed as a column vector, $\overrightarrow{PB} = \begin{bmatrix} 1.8 \\ 2.2 \end{bmatrix}$.

$|\overrightarrow{PB}| = \sqrt{1.8^2 + 2.2^2} = 2.8$ km

$\tan \alpha = \dfrac{1.8}{2.2} = 0.818 \implies \alpha = 39°$

$\overrightarrow{PB} = 2.8$ km bearing 039°

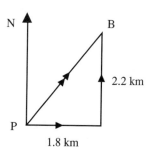

This result can be checked by making measurements on the map (remember that a side of a square represents 1 km).

Exercise B (answers p. 132)

1   Six-figure map references for places A, B, C, D are:

A 015392,   B 227461,   C 100260,   D 312329.

(a) Calculate the distance from C to B.

(b) Find the bearing of D from A.

(c) Find $\overrightarrow{BD}$ as a distance and bearing.

(d) What is the bearing of vector $\overrightarrow{DB}$?

(e) What may be said about $\overrightarrow{AB}$ and $\overrightarrow{CD}$?

2   The six-figure map reference for a town A is 214418. Town B is 12 km from A on a bearing of 120°. Calculate the map reference of B.

3   Calculate the distance and bearing of Ayton (grid reference 214300) from Botton (grid reference 318206).

C   Adding vectors (answers p. 132)

1D | There are two ways of giving a displacement – as a column vector or as a distance and bearing.

Do you really need two ways of describing the same thing?

Is one form of vector more useful than the other?

The following questions explore how you can combine vectors by addition, where, for example, one displacement is followed by another.

2   A police helicopter is monitoring traffic flow. Trouble spots are known to be at

X (026102),   Y (134154)   and   Z (185496).

(a) Write $\overrightarrow{XZ}$, $\overrightarrow{XY}$ and $\overrightarrow{YZ}$ as column vectors.

(b) Can you see any connection between $\overrightarrow{XZ}$, $\overrightarrow{XY}$ and $\overrightarrow{YZ}$?
     $\overrightarrow{XZ}$ is called the **resultant** of $\overrightarrow{XY}$ and $\overrightarrow{YZ}$.

(c) In what direction, and how far, does the helicopter fly in going from
     (i) X to Z   (ii) X to Y   (iii) Y to Z?

3 For any vector triangle, as shown, $\overrightarrow{AC}$ is called the resultant of $\overrightarrow{AB}$ and $\overrightarrow{BC}$.

Express $\overrightarrow{AB}$, $\overrightarrow{BC}$ and $\overrightarrow{AC}$ as column vectors. What do you notice?

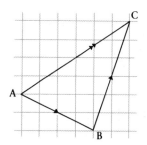

4 Find the resultant $\overrightarrow{AD}$ of these vectors:

$$\overrightarrow{AB} = \begin{bmatrix} 2 \\ 2 \end{bmatrix} \qquad \overrightarrow{BC} = \begin{bmatrix} 2 \\ 0 \end{bmatrix} \qquad \overrightarrow{CD} = \begin{bmatrix} 3 \\ -4 \end{bmatrix}$$

Using squared paper, draw a vector diagram to illustrate all four vectors.

5 Find the resultant $\overrightarrow{AD}$ of these vectors:

$$\overrightarrow{AE} = \begin{bmatrix} 3 \\ -4 \end{bmatrix} \qquad \overrightarrow{EF} = \begin{bmatrix} 2 \\ 2 \end{bmatrix} \qquad \overrightarrow{FD} = \begin{bmatrix} 2 \\ 0 \end{bmatrix}$$

Illustrate the vectors on the diagram used for question 4. What do you notice?

The **resultant** of a displacement from X to Y followed by a displacement from Y to Z is the displacement from X to Z.

Two vectors can be added by means of a scale drawing if they are drawn 'head to tail'.

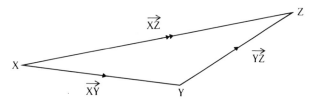

$$\overrightarrow{XY} + \overrightarrow{YZ} = \overrightarrow{XZ}$$

The same resultant displacement is obtained if the two displacement vectors are added in the other order.

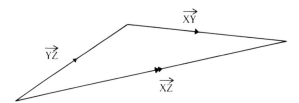

All that matters is that the 'head' of the first displacement vector you draw should be followed by the 'tail' of the next displacement vector.

To add together two vectors given in column vector form, add the x-components together and add the y-components together.

$$\begin{bmatrix} 2 \\ 3 \end{bmatrix} + \begin{bmatrix} 4 \\ -1 \end{bmatrix} = \begin{bmatrix} 6 \\ 2 \end{bmatrix}$$

The reason they add up in this way becomes clear if the vector diagram is drawn. The vectors form the sides of the triangle TUV.

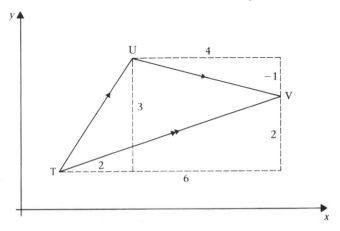

You should note that whereas $\overrightarrow{TU} + \overrightarrow{UV} = \overrightarrow{TV}$, it is not true that $TU + UV = TV$.

Example 5

Express $\overrightarrow{PQ}$ in terms of the vectors **a** and **b** shown in the diagram.

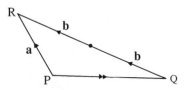

Solution

$$\overrightarrow{PQ} = \overrightarrow{PR} + \overrightarrow{RQ} \implies \overrightarrow{PQ} = \mathbf{a} - 2\mathbf{b}$$

Note that this book uses **bold** face to indicate vector quantities like **a** and **b**.

You could do this in your work by underlining, writing $\underline{a}$ or $\underline{a}$.

Exercise C (answers p. 133)

1 Add the vectors $\begin{bmatrix} 3 \\ -1 \end{bmatrix}$ and $\begin{bmatrix} -2 \\ 4 \end{bmatrix}$. Draw them and their resultant and show how they form a closed triangle.

2 For each of the following examples, write the vector $\overrightarrow{PQ}$ in terms of **u** and **v**.

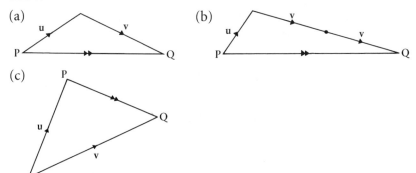

(a)

(b)

(c)

3 Four displacement vectors have a resultant of $\begin{bmatrix} 10 \\ -2 \end{bmatrix}$. If three of them are $\begin{bmatrix} -2 \\ -3 \end{bmatrix}$, $\begin{bmatrix} 5 \\ -7 \end{bmatrix}$ and $\begin{bmatrix} 16 \\ 4 \end{bmatrix}$, find the missing vector.

4 A helicopter flies from its base A (025105) to B (105155) and then to C (195400). While the helicopter is flying from B to C, a second helicopter flies parallel to it, travelling from A to D where the distances AD and BC are equal.

   (a) Express $\overrightarrow{BC}$ and $\overrightarrow{AD}$ as column vectors.

   (b) Find the map reference for D.

   (c) Find $\overrightarrow{AB}$ and $\overrightarrow{DC}$. What shape is ABCD?

D Using vectors (answers p. 133)

Two vectors may be added or subtracted by scale drawing or using column vectors. A third method is to draw a rough diagram then use the cosine and sine rules.

Example 6

One boat of a fishing fleet sails 4 km from a port in a direction 049° to investigate the prospects of good catches. The rest of the fleet travels to its usual fishing ground, 10 km from the same port in a direction 120°. In what direction does the single boat have to sail to rejoin the fleet and what distance will it cover?

Solution

Let P be the port, S the single boat and F the rest of the fleet.

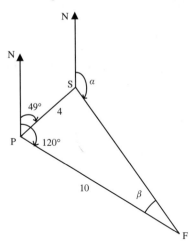

Method 1
The diagram has been drawn to the scale [1 cm : 2 km]. By measurement, SF = 4.7 cm, representing 9.4 km, and α = 143°.

Method 2

$$\overrightarrow{PS} = \begin{bmatrix} 4\sin 49° \\ 4\cos 49° \end{bmatrix} = \begin{bmatrix} 3.02 \\ 2.62 \end{bmatrix}, \qquad \overrightarrow{PF} = \begin{bmatrix} 8.66 \\ -5.00 \end{bmatrix}$$

$$\overrightarrow{PS} + \overrightarrow{SF} = \overrightarrow{PF} \implies \overrightarrow{SF} = \begin{bmatrix} 8.66 \\ -5.00 \end{bmatrix} - \begin{bmatrix} 3.02 \\ 2.62 \end{bmatrix} = \begin{bmatrix} 5.64 \\ -7.62 \end{bmatrix}$$

The column vector is now converted back to a distance and bearing.

$$|\overrightarrow{SF}| = \sqrt{5.64^2 + 7.62^2} = 9.48$$

$$\tan \gamma = \frac{7.62}{5.64} \implies \gamma = 53.5°$$

Bearing is 90° + 53.5° = 143.5°.

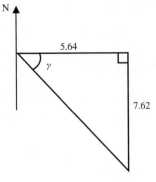

Method 3
In the original diagram, angle SPF = 120° − 49° = 71°.

$$SF^2 = 4^2 + 10^2 - 2 \times 4 \times 10 \times \cos 71° \text{ from the cosine rule}$$

$$SF = 9.48$$

The sine rule now gives $\dfrac{\sin \beta}{4} = \dfrac{\sin 71°}{9.48}$, so $\beta = 23.5°$

$\alpha = 120° + 23.5° = 143.5°$

All three methods show that to rejoin the fleet the single boat should sail on a bearing of 143° for a distance of 9.5 km. Drawing is less accurate than the other methods but this is not often important in practice.

H/W **Exercise D** (answers p. 133)

(You may like to answer some questions by more than one method.)

1   An aircraft A develops an engine fault when it is 83 km due west of an airport P. Another airport Q is 100 km from P on a bearing 315°. Which airport is closer to the aircraft, and by how much?

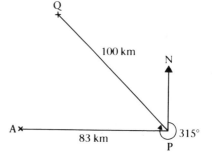

2   A ship S, having sailed 20 km from port P in a direction 127°, dropped anchor and sent an SOS for a seriously ill passenger to be lifted off. At that instant an air–sea rescue helicopter H was 5 km due east of P. In which direction and for what distance did the helicopter have to fly in order to reach the ship?

3   Storm Head Light is 4.7 km east of Black Cap Light. A fishing boat is observed at 2:15 a.m. due north of Storm Head Light. If the boat progresses on a bearing of 322° at 9.0 km h^{-1}, at what time will it be observed due north of Black Cap Light?

4   A hill walker is injured when she is 6 km north-west of Horton. The rescue helicopter is based 30 km from Horton on a bearing of 078°. In what direction and for what distance does the helicopter have to fly in order to reach the injured walker?

5   [1 knot is a speed of 1 nautical mile per hour, a nautical mile being 1.15 land miles.]

    HMS *Battledore* leaves port at 14:15 and sails at 15 knots on a bearing 119° for 24 minutes, then changes course to bearing 343°, on which the ship remains. At 14:30 HMS *Shuttlecock* leaves the same port and sails on a bearing 205° at 12 knots until 15:00 at which time its engines cease to work. How far apart are the two ships at 15:00? How long will it take HMS *Battledore* to get to HMS *Shuttlecock* at 20 knots? On what bearing must HMS *Battledore* proceed?

E Position and displacement (answers p. 134)

The word 'displacement' has been used to describe a distance moved in a certain direction. It can also be used to define a position.

The displacement from the origin to a point is called the **position vector** of the point.

Here the movement implied by the use of the word 'displacement' is hypothetical; it can be thought of as the distance and direction of a possible journey from the origin, even though no actual movement takes place.

The diagram shows a fishing boat F and a marker buoy B. Viewed from a lighthouse which is taken as the origin, their position vectors are $\begin{bmatrix} -2 \\ 5 \end{bmatrix}$ and $\begin{bmatrix} 4 \\ 3 \end{bmatrix}$.

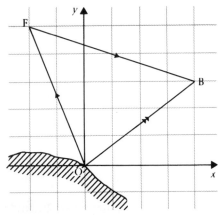

Note that $\begin{bmatrix} 4 \\ 3 \end{bmatrix} - \begin{bmatrix} -2 \\ 5 \end{bmatrix} = \begin{bmatrix} 6 \\ -2 \end{bmatrix}$

and that $\overrightarrow{FB} = \begin{bmatrix} 6 \\ -2 \end{bmatrix}$.

Displacement $\overrightarrow{FB}$ = Position vector of B − Position vector of F,
$$\overrightarrow{FB} = \overrightarrow{OB} - \overrightarrow{OF}$$

Example 7

A plane moves from the point with position vector $\begin{bmatrix} 3 \\ 6 \end{bmatrix}$ km to the point with position vector $\begin{bmatrix} 7 \\ -3 \end{bmatrix}$ km. Find its displacement.

Solution

Displacement = New position vector − Old position vector

$$= \begin{bmatrix} 7 \\ -3 \end{bmatrix} - \begin{bmatrix} 3 \\ 6 \end{bmatrix} = \begin{bmatrix} 4 \\ -9 \end{bmatrix} \text{ km}$$

Displacement = Change in position vector

H/W **Exercise E** (answers p. 134)

1   A boat travels down a winding channel. Its original position vector was $\begin{bmatrix} 5.7 \\ 2.6 \end{bmatrix}$ km and its journey can be described by the successive

displacement vectors $\begin{bmatrix} 0.9 \\ 0.2 \end{bmatrix}$, $\begin{bmatrix} 1.4 \\ -0.7 \end{bmatrix}$ and $\begin{bmatrix} 1.2 \\ 0.5 \end{bmatrix}$ km.

   (a) Find its new position vector.
   (b) What is its total displacement?
   (c) How far has the boat travelled?

2   A coastguard has position vector $\begin{bmatrix} 7.4 \\ -3.3 \end{bmatrix}$ km and a boat has position

   vector $\begin{bmatrix} 2.1 \\ 8.4 \end{bmatrix}$ km. The boat travels 11.5 km in the direction 068°.

   Draw a rough sketch and calculate the displacement from the coastguard to the boat.

3   Complete the following table.

	(a)	(b)	(c)	(d)
Original position vector	$\begin{bmatrix} 200 \\ 90 \end{bmatrix}$	$\begin{bmatrix} 7 \\ -7 \end{bmatrix}$	$\begin{bmatrix} -32 \\ 16 \end{bmatrix}$	
New position			$\begin{bmatrix} -15 \\ -4 \end{bmatrix}$	$\begin{bmatrix} -10 \\ -8 \end{bmatrix}$
Displacement	$\begin{bmatrix} 126 \\ -9 \end{bmatrix}$	$\begin{bmatrix} 66 \\ -74 \end{bmatrix}$		$\begin{bmatrix} 78 \\ 254 \end{bmatrix}$

After working through this chapter you should

1   be aware that displacement is a vector quantity and has both magnitude and direction

2   know that the magnitude of $\overrightarrow{AB}$ is the distance from A to B and is written as $|\overrightarrow{AB}|$ or AB

3   understand that a column vectors can describe either a displacement or a position vector

4   be able to convert column vectors to distance and bearing form and vice versa

5   be able to convert six-figure map references to coordinates and vice versa

6   know that vectors can be added 'head to tail' in either order, i.e.
$$\mathbf{a} + \mathbf{b} = \mathbf{b} + \mathbf{a}$$

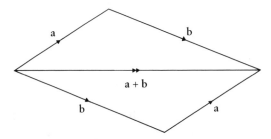

and can be added as column vectors, for example

$$\begin{bmatrix} 3 \\ 2 \end{bmatrix} + \begin{bmatrix} 5 \\ -2 \end{bmatrix} = \begin{bmatrix} 8 \\ 0 \end{bmatrix}$$

7   know that displacement is change in position vector and that

Original position vector + Displacement = Final position vector

4 Velocity

A Speed or velocity? (answers p. 134)

The speed of an object is simply a measure of how fast it is travelling. In everyday language, 'velocity' is often used in this way as well. However, mathematicians and scientists use the word 'velocity' in the special sense of meaning speed *and* direction.

1 Consider a car travelling along a winding road.

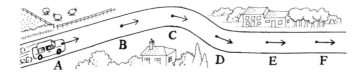

Points A to F show the car's position at 10-second intervals. Over what parts of the journey is

(a) the speed constant (b) the velocity constant?

Speed is an example of a scalar quantity; it can, for example, be read from the speedometer of a car without reference to the direction of travel.

> Velocity is a vector having the same magnitude as speed but pointing in the direction of motion.

Two cars travelling at 40 kilometres per hour (40 km h^{-1}), one going north and the other going east, have the same speed but different velocities. The velocities can be represented by arrows drawn to scale in appropriate directions, or by column vectors.

$$\begin{bmatrix} 0 \\ 40 \end{bmatrix} \quad \text{or} \quad 40 \text{ km h}^{-1} \uparrow \qquad \begin{bmatrix} 40 \\ 0 \end{bmatrix} \quad \text{or} \quad 40 \text{ km h}^{-1} \longrightarrow$$

Just as 'average speed' means the **equivalent constant speed**, so 'average velocity' means the **equivalent constant velocity**.

2 The village of Northaven is 30 kilometres due
north of Southlea. One car travels from Southlea
to Northaven at an average speed of 60 km h^{-1}. A
second car does the same journey with an average
velocity of 60 km h^{-1} due north.

What precisely do the sentences above imply about
the motion of these two cars? Do they in fact mean
the same thing?

The ideas of equivalent constant speed and
equivalent constant velocity are summarised as
follows.

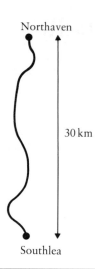

Northaven

30 km

Southlea

$$\text{Average speed} \quad = \frac{\text{Total distance travelled}}{\text{Time taken}}$$

$$\text{Average velocity} = \frac{\text{Change in position vector}}{\text{Time taken}}$$

Example 1

Susan walks 2 km in half an hour along a road which runs north and
then runs back halfway along her route in 10 minutes.

What are her average speed and her average velocity for the whole
journey?

Solution

The total time for the whole hour is 40 minutes $= \frac{2}{3}$ hour, while the
total distance for the whole journey is 3 km.

Average speed $= 3 \div \frac{2}{3}\,\text{km h}^{-1} = \frac{9}{2}\,\text{km h}^{-1} = 4.5\,\text{km h}^{-1}$

Displacement $= 1$ km north

Average velocity $= 1 \div \frac{2}{3}\,\text{km h}^{-1}\,\text{north} = 1.5\,\text{km h}^{-1}\,\text{north}$

Exercise A (answers p. 135)

1 A car travels 20 km at 40 km h^{-1} and then returns along the same
route at 80 km h^{-1}. What is the average speed for the total journey?

2 A car travels 30 km at 30 km h^{-1} and then increases its speed to
60 km h^{-1}. How far does it travel on the second stage of its journey if
its average speed is 45 km h^{-1}?

3 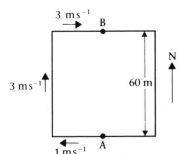 A and B are the mid-points of opposite edges of a square field. Melissa travels from A to B, around the edge of the field, with speeds as shown. What are her average speed and average velocity?

4 If an object is travelling with a constant speed, then is it necessarily travelling with constant velocity? If it travels with constant velocity, is it necessarily travelling with constant speed? Give reasons and examples.

5 State, with reasons, what can be said about the average speed of a car which travels with an average velocity of 50 km h^{-1} due east.

6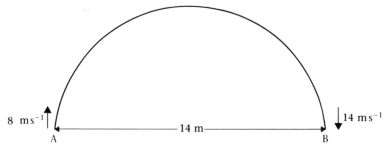

A particle moves on a semicircular path, its speed increasing uniformly with time from 8 m s^{-1} to 14 m s^{-1}.

(a) What is the average speed of the particle and how many seconds does it take to complete this path?

(b) At what point on the path does the particle's speed equal 11 m s^{-1}?

(c) What is its average velocity in travelling from A to B?

7E Because of engine problems, a racing car completes one lap of a race at an average speed of only 40 km h^{-1}. At what speed must it complete a second lap so that its average speed for both laps is

(a) 60 km h^{-1} (b) 80 km h^{-1}?

B Straight line motion (answers p. 136)

Even for motion in a straight line, there is a distinction between distance and displacement and between speed and velocity.

Velocity in the direction of positive displacement will be positive and in the direction of negative displacement will be negative.

Speed cannot be negative.

If the particle at P has a *velocity* of 8 m s^{-1} then it is moving from left to right. If its *velocity* is −8 m s^{-1} then it is moving from right to left. The *speed* of the particle would be 8 m s^{-1} in both cases; the speed gives you no idea of the *direction* in which the particle is moving. If you want to know about direction of motion, you must deal with velocities.

1 A ball is projected so that it rolls up an inclined track and then rolls down again. Its (time, displacement) graph is shown below.

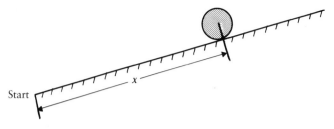

(You may wish to tackle this as a practical and substitute your own data.)

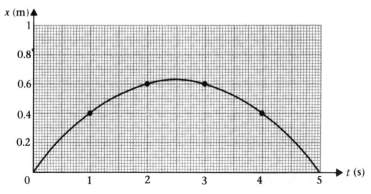

Plot a $\left(t, \dfrac{dx}{dt}\right)$ graph, either by measuring gradients or by finding the

equation of the (time, displacement) graph and using calculus to

find $\dfrac{dx}{dt}$.

(a) What do your graphs tell you about the motion?

(b) What does the area between the $\left(t, \dfrac{dx}{dt}\right)$ graph and the *t*-axis

represent?

(c) What does it mean if the area is below the t-axis?

(d) What is the velocity of the ball after these times?

   (i) 1 second   (ii) 4 seconds

(e) What is the average velocity of the ball in these time intervals?

   (i) during the 2nd second   (ii) during the first 5 seconds

---

The displacement from the origin x and velocity $\dfrac{dx}{dt}$ used in describing straight line motion are vector quantities. One direction of the line is chosen to be positive.

The area under a $\left(t, \dfrac{dx}{dt}\right)$ graph represents displacement. If the area is beneath the axis, the displacement is negative.

Example 2

(a) Describe the motion illustrated by the two graphs given below.

(b) Find, a, T and the total distance travelled.

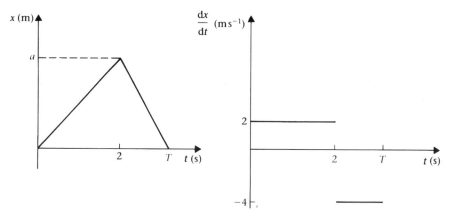

Solution

(a) The object travels away from its starting position with a constant velocity of $2 \ \mathrm{m\,s^{-1}}$. When $t = 2$, it changes its velocity to $-4 \ \mathrm{m\,s^{-1}}$ and returns to its starting position when $t = T$.

(b) The areas under the $\left(t, \dfrac{dx}{dt}\right)$ graph give the displacement during the interval of time.

The (t, x) graph shows that the position vector increases in magnitude from 0 to a in 2 seconds and becomes 0 again after T seconds.

The $\left(t, \dfrac{dx}{dt}\right)$ graph shows that the displacement after the first
2 seconds is 4 metres (the area under the line) so $a = 4$ and the
total distance travelled is 8 metres.

The 4 metres back take 1 second at 4 m s^{-1}, so $T = 3$.

Example 3

A particle P moves along a straight line so that its displacement
x metres from its initial position at time t seconds is

$$x = t(t-1).$$

(a) (i)   Find the velocity of the particle when $t = 4$.
    (ii) Find the direction in which the particle is moving at this
        time.

(b) Find the velocity of the particle when it first returns to the starting
position.

(c) Describe the motion of the particle.

Solution

(a) (i) $x = t^2 - t \implies \text{velocity } v = \dfrac{dx}{dt} = 2t - 1$

    When $t = 4$, the velocity is 7 m s^{-1}.
    (ii) The velocity is $+7 \text{ m s}^{-1}$, so the particle is moving from left to
        right along the line.

(b) The particle is at its starting position when $x = 0$.

$$0 = t(t-1) \implies t = 0 \text{ or } t = 1$$

The particle first returns to its starting position when $t = 1$. At this
time it has a velocity of 1 m s^{-1}.

(c) When $t = 0$, $v = -1 \text{ m s}^{-1}$. The particle is moving left at 1 m s^{-1}.
$v = 0$ when $2t - 1 = 0$, i.e. when $t = \frac{1}{2}$.

When $t > \frac{1}{2}$, $v > 0$ and the particle is moving to the right.

The particle starts moving left with a speed of 1 m s^{-1}; it slows
down and momentarily stops after $\frac{1}{2}$ second, changing direction to
move back toward its initial position. It passes through its initial
position again when $t = 1$ second, moving right at 1 m s^{-1}. It
continues to move away to the right, increasing its speed as it does
so. It does not change direction again.

Exercise B (answers p. 136)

1 The motion of an object is represented by the graphs shown below.

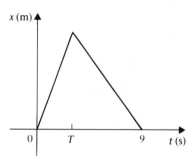 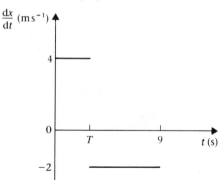

What is:

(a) the value of T (b) the distance covered after 9 seconds

(c) the displacement after 9 seconds?

2 A child throws a ball up from the top of a tower. The displacement x metres from its initial position after t seconds is given by the formula $x = 6t - 5t^2$.

(a) By using calculus, find the velocity of the ball after $\frac{1}{4}$ second and after 2 seconds.

(b) Find the average velocity of the ball for the first 3 seconds.

3 It is 10 km from A to B. Mary cycles from A to B, starting at 12 noon, at a steady speed of 15 km h^{-1} and then immediately turns and comes back to A at a speed of $7\frac{1}{2}$ km h^{-1}. John sets off on foot from B at noon and walks at a steady speed of 3 km h^{-1} to A.

(a) Draw (t, x) graphs of their motions on the same diagram, where t is the time and x is the distance in kilometres from A.

(b) At what times t_1 and t_2 do Mary and John pass each other and how far are they from A at these times?

(c) At what time between t_1 and t_2 are they the greatest distance apart?

4 Part of a (t, y) graph is shown for a ball which is dropped from a height of 10 metres onto the floor.

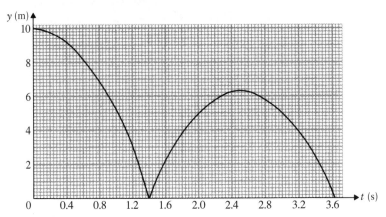

(a) Sketch the $\left(t, \dfrac{dy}{dt}\right)$ graph.

(b) Explain what happens when $t = 1.4$.

(c) Sketch a continuation of the (t, y) graph after $t = 3.6$.

(d) What is the ball's speed when $t = 1$?

C Change in velocity (answers p. 137)

1D Suppose that three clockwork toy cars are each moving with a constant speed of 30 cm s^{-1} on the surface of a floor mat. The mat is then pulled across the floor at a speed of 40 cm s^{-1}.

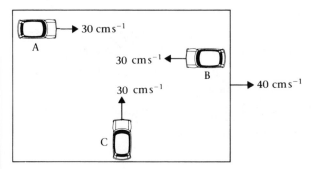

(a) Find the new velocities of the cars.

(b) What is the change in velocity of each car?

(c) What relationship is there between the initial velocity of each car and its final velocity?

When an object moves from point P to point Q, its change in position is simply the vector $\overrightarrow{PQ}$.

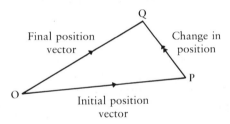

| Initial position vector | + | Change in position vector | = | Final position vector |

Adding vectors 'head to tail' leads to a similar result for velocities.

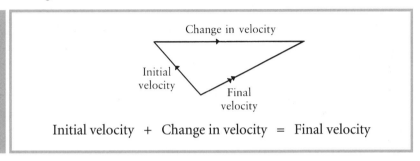

Initial velocity + Change in velocity = Final velocity

Example 4

If the initial velocity of a body is 6 m s^{-1} on a bearing of 320° and the final velocity of the body is 10 m s^{-1} due north, what is its change in velocity?

Solution

You have a choice of methods for solving this problem:

Solution by drawing (or trigonometry)
Change in velocity = 6.6 m s^{-1} bearing 036°

Solution by components
Initial velocity + Change in velocity = Final velocity

Change in velocity = Final velocity − Initial velocity

$$\text{Change in velocity} = \begin{bmatrix} 0 \\ 10 \end{bmatrix} - \begin{bmatrix} 6\sin 320° \\ 6\cos 320° \end{bmatrix} \approx \begin{bmatrix} 3.9 \\ 5.4 \end{bmatrix}$$

Now $\sqrt{3.9^2 + 5.4^2} = 6.7$ and $\tan^{-1}\dfrac{3.9}{5.4} = 35.8°$, which

are consistent with the previous answer.

Scale 1 cm : 2 m s^{-1}

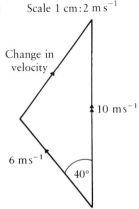

Exercise C (answers p. 137)

1   What is the change in velocity when an object's velocity changes from:

(a) 5 m s^{-1} due east to 8 m s^{-1} due west

(b) 5 m s^{-1} due west to 8 m s^{-1} due east

(c) 5 m s^{-1} due east to 8 m s^{-1} due north?

2   A boat is steered north-west at a speed of 4 km h^{-1}. It then changes course to travel north-east at a speed of 6 km h^{-1}. Find the change in velocity of the boat.

3   An aeroplane has velocity $\begin{bmatrix} 200 \\ 10 \end{bmatrix} \text{ km h}^{-1}$. It changes its velocity by $\begin{bmatrix} -30 \\ 40 \end{bmatrix} \text{ km h}^{-1}$. What is the final velocity of the aeroplane?

4   What is the change in velocity of a particle when its velocity changes from $\begin{bmatrix} 0 \\ -4 \end{bmatrix} \text{ m s}^{-1}$ to $\begin{bmatrix} 6 \\ 2 \end{bmatrix} \text{ m s}^{-1}$?

5   An aeroplane is travelling at 200 km h^{-1} on a bearing 050°. A wind then blows so that the aeroplane ends up travelling at 200 km h^{-1} on a bearing 054°.

Find the velocity of the wind.

D Resultant velocity (answers p. 138)

As you have seen, the idea of change of velocity is closely connected to that of the resultant velocity of an object and a moving medium, such as a floor mat or a wind.

Example 5

A boat is steered with velocity $\begin{bmatrix} 0 \\ -3 \end{bmatrix} \text{ km h}^{-1}$ in a current running at $\begin{bmatrix} -5 \\ 0 \end{bmatrix} \text{ km h}^{-1}$. Find the resultant velocity of the boat in these forms.

(a)   As a column vector   (b)   In speed and bearing form

Solution

(a)

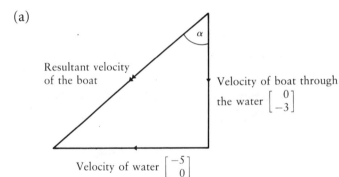

$$\text{Resultant velocity} = \begin{bmatrix} 0 \\ -3 \end{bmatrix} + \begin{bmatrix} -5 \\ 0 \end{bmatrix} = \begin{bmatrix} -5 \\ -3 \end{bmatrix} \text{km h}^{-1}$$

(b) Speed $= \sqrt{5^2 + 3^2} \approx 5.8 \text{ km h}^{-1}$

$\tan \alpha = \frac{5}{3} \Rightarrow \alpha \approx 59°$

The bearing is $180° + 59° = 239°$.

Now consider a similar but more open-ended question.

You want to cross a river in a boat. At what angle should you steer and how long will it take you to cross?

Set up a model

Take a simple case first.

Let the river be 100 m wide and its speed of flow be 1 m s^{-1}.

Suppose you set off from a point P at an angle α with the bank.

Assume that you can row at 2 m s^{-1} and want to land directly opposite.

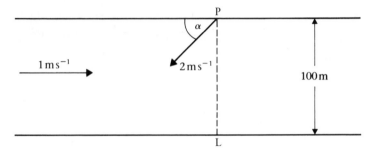

Analyse the problem

You know that your resultant velocity is

Velocity through the water + Velocity of the water

From the vector triangle, $\cos \alpha = \frac{1}{2} \Rightarrow \alpha = 60°$

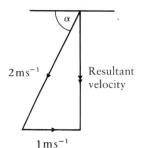

You must row at an angle of 60° to the bank.

Resultant speed $= \sqrt{2^2 - 1^2} = 1.73 \text{ m s}^{-1}$

Time taken $= \dfrac{100}{1.73} = 57.8$ seconds

Interpret/validate

Assuming that you can row at a constant speed for almost a minute, you should reach the other side of the river at a spot opposite your departure point P. If you aim even further upstream you will land upstream.

1 A canoe can travel at 4 m s^{-1} in still water. How long would it take to complete the circuit shown with a constant current of 3 m s^{-1} flowing in the direction indicated?

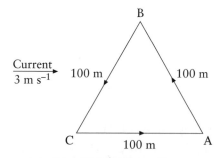

(a) Part of the vector diagram for the leg from A to B is shown. The length of the resultant velocity vector is not yet known. How can you complete the vector triangle?

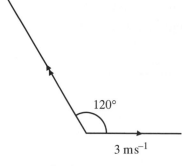

(b) Do you think an experienced canoeist could steer the best course?

(c) Find the journey time from A to B and for the whole course.

Exercise D (answers p. 138)

1   A woman walks at 2 m s^{-1} across the deck of a boat. The boat is moving at 8 m s^{-1}. Find the resultant speed of the woman.

2   A girl wishes to paddle her canoe across a river to the nearest point on the opposite bank. If she can paddle at 1.5 m s^{-1} in still water and the river is running at 1 m s^{-1}, in what direction should she point the canoe? If the river is 100 m wide, how long will it take her to cross?

    Comment on any assumptions you have made.

3   A river is 100 m wide and flows between two parallel banks at a speed of 3 m s^{-1}. If you point a canoe directly across the river and paddle at 4 m s^{-1}, how far downstream will you end up on the opposite bank?

    How long will it take you to cross?

4   Crossing the same river as in question 3, if you wish to end up directly opposite your start point, at what angle should you point and paddle the canoe?

    How long will it take you to cross?

5   Again crossing the river in question 3, you point the canoe at 45° to the bank and into the current. Where will you end up on the other side? How long will it take you?

6   A plane with an airspeed of 250 km h^{-1} has to fly from a town A to a town B, 100 km due east of A, in a wind blowing from 030° at 50 km h^{-1}. Find, by drawing, the direction in which the plane must be headed and the time taken.

7E A river flows with a speed of 1.5 km h^{-1}. Find in what direction a swimmer, whose speed through the water is 2.5 km h^{-1}, should start in order to cross at 30° downstream to the bank. Find his resultant speed.

E   A modelling exercise (answers p. 139)

1   You are the pilot of a light aircraft which is capable of cruising at a steady speed in still air. You have enough fuel on board to last four hours. What is the maximum distance you can fly from your base and still return home safely?

Consider what factors are relevant:

- the velocity of the plane
- the wind velocity, etc.

Make assumptions that will simplify the problem. For example, you could assume that the wind velocity is in a direction parallel to the velocity of the plane.

It might also help to make estimates of any relevant quantities and solve the problem for these values before you refine and generalise your model.

After working through this chapter you should

1   know that speed and distance are scalar quantities

2   know that velocity and displacement are vector quantities which have both magnitude and direction

3   be able to find the equivalent constant velocity from

$$\text{Average velocity} = \frac{\text{Change in position vector}}{\text{Time taken}}$$

4   know that

Initial velocity + Change in velocity = Final velocity

and that this relationship can be represented in a vector triangle

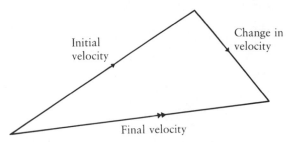

5   be able to find changes in velocity and resultant velocities using either a vector triangle or column vectors as appropriate

6   know that for motion in a straight line, $v = \dfrac{\mathrm{d}x}{\mathrm{d}t}$.

5 Changes in motion

A Momentum – the 'quantity of motion' (answers p. 140)

1D | What makes a moving object easy or difficult to bring to rest?
Consider different situations in which things at rest are set in motion. What makes it easy or difficult to move them?

First thoughts, together with everyday experience and observation, tell you that the faster something is travelling, the harder it is to stop. Similarly, the faster you wish something to go, the harder it is to achieve that speed.

You should be aware that some measure of the quantity of the object is relevant. Clearly, it is not just the volume (compare a shot-putter's shot and a beach ball) and not just the concentration of matter, or density of the object – but a combination of the two. This combination is called the mass of the object.

2D

What do you understand by the word 'mass'?

How can you compare the masses of different objects?
Is it helpful to think in terms of the size or volume of the objects?
Can you use the weights of objects to compare their masses?

The **mass** of an object is the amount of matter it contains. Masses of objects of the same density can therefore be compared by simply measuring their volumes. The unit of mass, the **kilogram**, is now defined as the mass of a certain block of platinum–iridium alloy that is kept at Sèvres in France. It used to be defined as the mass of 1 litre of pure water at the temperature of its greatest density (4 °C). Unfortunately a mistake was made and the kilogram is actually now the mass of 1000.028 cm^3 of water!

The pull of the Earth on an object is proportional to its mass and so, to compare the masses of objects of different densities, we can compare the pulls the Earth exerts upon them, i.e. their weights. Greengrocers' spring balances are calibrated in kilograms as if they measured mass, but they really measure weight. Six kilograms of apples would still have mass six kilograms on the Moon but such a spring balance would read only approximately 1 kg because of the much smaller gravitational pull of the Moon.

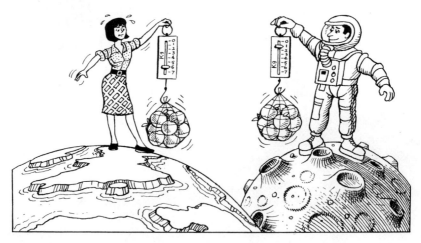

The mass of an object is the amount of matter it contains.
1 kilogram has been defined as the mass of 1 litre of pure water.

To familiarise yourself with what Sir Isaac Newton called the 'quantities of motion' you should try the following simple experiments.

3 Place a block on a table and roll a snooker ball slowly along the table towards it.

   (a) When the ball hits the block, what happens

      (i) to the ball   (ii) to the block?

   (b) Now use a table tennis ball. Try to make it travel at about the same speed. What happens now?

   (c) Repeat (a) and (b) using a higher velocity for the balls.

4 (a) Get a friend to drop the snooker ball from a height, allowing you to catch it in your hand. Describe what you feel as the height is increased in 50 cm steps from 50 cm to 2 metres.

   (b) Repeat the experiment with the table tennis ball.

   (c) What you feel is what Newton called the fundamental 'quantity of motion'. What do you think are the important factors which make up this quantity?

5 Which do you think has more 'quantity of motion', a 4 tonne lorry travelling at 1 ms^{-1} or an 800 kg car travelling at 5 m s^{-1}?

The fundamental 'quantity of motion' seems to depend upon both mass and velocity. The following experiments investigate further the nature of this quantity in the context of collisions. It is surprising, when you consider how wild and apparently disordered collisions can be, that there should be any simple connection between the situations before and after the collision.

Equipment
- Straight section of track
- Two trucks of equal total mass
- Assorted masses which can be placed on either truck

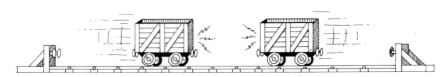

6 (a) Set up the two trucks so that they will bounce apart. What happens if one truck is propelled towards the other stationary truck? Repeat with various masses on each truck and write down your conclusions.

   (b) Set up the two trucks so that they will stick together on impact. Try different conditions as in (a).

The fundamental 'quantity of motion' of an object is the product of its mass and velocity. This quantity of motion is called **momentum**.

$$\text{Momentum} = \text{Mass} \times \text{Velocity}$$

An object of mass 0.1 kg and moving with a speed of 2 m s^{-1} has momentum of 0.2 kg m s^{-1}. Momentum is a vector quantity and you should picture it as a vector of magnitude 0.2 kg m s^{-1} in the direction of the object's velocity.

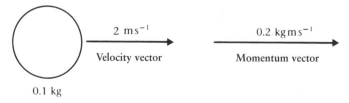

0.1 kg

Exercise A (answers p. 141)

1 Which of the following objects have the *same* momentum:
   (a) a 3 kg shot rolled along the ground at 5 m s^{-1} in a northerly direction
   (b) a 6 kg shot rolled along the ground at 2.5 m s^{-1} in an easterly direction
   (c) a 3 kg shot rolled along the ground at 5 m s^{-1} in an easterly direction?

2 A woman of mass 70 kg has a velocity which can be represented by the vector $\begin{bmatrix} 3 \\ 4 \end{bmatrix}$ m s^{-1}, the components being in the directions east and north respectively.
   Find her momentum in vector form and calculate its magnitude and direction.

3 Sketch pairs of vectors to represent the momenta of the objects described below, giving reasons for the size of the vectors:
   (a) a car of mass one tonne moving north at 90 km h^{-1} and a ten tonne lorry travelling east at 30 km h^{-1}
   (b) a speedboat cutting across the bows of a ferry
   (c) a jeep racing a rhinoceros.

B Conservation of momentum (answers p. 141)

In the collisions investigated in Section A, you may have observed that the total momentum after a collision was about the same as the total momentum before the collision. We take this to be exactly true.

When total momentum is unchanged, mathematicians and physicists speak of the **conservation of momentum**.

Suppose an object moving with speed 2 m s^{-1} collides with a stationary object as shown below.

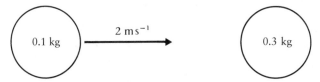

Three of the possible situations immediately after the collision are as follows.

(a) The lighter object might rebound.

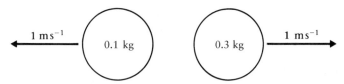

(b) The objects might stick together.

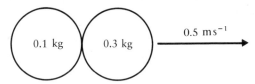

(c) The blow might be a glancing one.

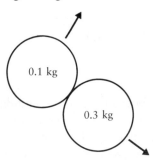

In each case, the momenta of the two objects after the collision add up vectorially (i.e. 'head to tail') to the original momentum of 0.2 kg m s^{-1}.

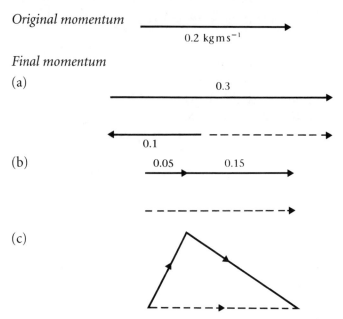

Original momentum

0.2 kg m s^{-1}

Final momentum

(a)

0.3

0.1

(b)

0.05   0.15

(c)

In each case, the final momenta add up to 0.2 kg m s^{-1}. The total momentum has not been changed by the collision.

> The law of conservation of momentum.
>
> If no external forces act during a collision or explosion, the total momentum of the system is conserved.

The law of conservation of momentum is remarkable – not only is it simple but it applies to many different types of interaction. The law applies equally to the motion of subatomic particles and to the motion of railway trucks. Rocket propulsion is just one practical application of this important law.

You can use conservation of momentum to help predict velocities after a collision. This idea is illustrated in Examples 1 and 2.

Example 1

Eddie, travelling on a toboggan at 5 m s^{-1}, collides with Louise who is travelling on her toboggan at 3 m s^{-1} in the same direction. Eddie and his toboggan have a total mass of 60 kg while Louise and her toboggan have a total mass of 40 kg. The toboggans interlock and move on together. What is their speed immediately after the collision?

Solution

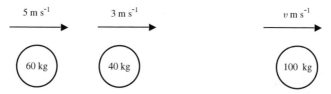

Initial momentum $= 60 \times 5 + 40 \times 3 = 420$ kg m s^{-1}.

Final momentum $= 100v$ kg m s^{-1}, where v m s^{-1} is the final velocity.
Conservation of momentum gives $100v = 420$,

$$v = 4.2$$

It has been assumed that *all* of the 100 kg moves with the same velocity
just after the collision. This is *not* a reasonable assumption as the
motions of Louise and Eddie will differ initially from those of their
toboggans. However, if they remain on their toboggans and if friction
has no appreciable effect, then the motion will soon settle down into
one of a uniform speed of approximately 4.2 m s^{-1}.

Example 2

Two bodies, of masses 2.5 kg and 5 kg, are moving in a horizontal
plane, with respective velocities 3 m s^{-1} south and 4 m s^{-1} west, when
they collide and coalesce. Find the subsequent speed of the compound
body.

Solution

The total momentum before (and
after) the collision can be found by
adding the vectors shown.

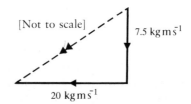

The length of the resultant can be found using Pythagoras' theorem.
The momentum afterwards is 21.4 kg m s^{-1}. Since the combined mass
is 7.5 kg, the subsequent speed is

$$\frac{21.4}{7.5} \approx 2.85 \text{ m s}^{-1}$$

Exercise B (answers p. 141)

1   In each of the situations below, find the velocity of B after the collision.

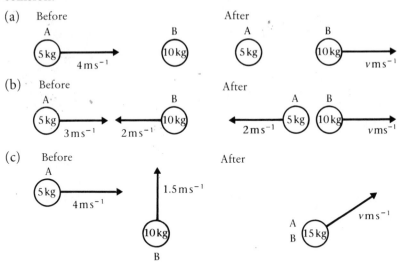

2   A car hit a parked van and after the collision the two vehicles became locked together and skidded to a stop. From the skid marks it was estimated that just after the impact the common velocity of the two vehicles was 7 m s^{-1}. If the total mass of the van and its load was 2000 kg and the mass of the car and its passengers was 1200 kg, what was the speed of the car just before impact?

3   A body A, of mass 3 kg, moving with a speed of 4 m s^{-1}, collides with a stationary body B, of mass 2 kg. After the collision A continues to move in its original direction with a speed of 2 m s^{-1}. What is the velocity of B after the collision?

4   A body P, of mass 2 kg, moving with a speed of 5 m s^{-1}, collides with a body Q which is approaching P in the same straight line, travelling in the opposite direction with a speed of 4 m s^{-1}. After the collision, both P and Q reverse their motion in the same straight line with respective speeds of 1 m s^{-1} and 2 m s^{-1}. Find the mass of Q.

5   Two bodies, of masses 3 kg and 4 kg, are each moving in a horizontal plane with a speed of 5 m s^{-1}, the first in direction 030° and the second in direction 120°. After collision, the body of mass 4 kg moves in its original direction but with a reduced speed of 3 m s^{-1}. Find, by means of a drawing, the velocity of the 3 kg mass after the collision.

6   A snooker ball of mass 0.15 kg moving at 0.6 m s^{-1} hits a stationary ball of the same mass. It is deflected through 40° and the speed is reduced to 0.2 m s^{-1}. Find the speed and direction of the second ball immediately after the impact.

C Change in momentum (answers p. 142)

You have seen that momentum is the fundamental 'quantity of motion'. We therefore measure 'changes in motion' by calculating the **change in momentum.**

Changes in momentum can be sudden, as in the collisions of Section A. You can also observe gradual changes in momentum as when an apple falls to the ground.

In the collision of Example 1 on p. 58, Louise and her toboggan (total mass 40 kg) increased speed from 3 m s^{-1} to 4.2 m s^{-1}. Their momentum increased by $40 \times 4.2 - 40 \times 3 = 48$ kg m s^{-1}.

1D Find the change in momentum for Eddie and his toboggan in Example 1. What do you notice? Can you explain why this should happen?

2 (a) Release a ball down a graduated ramp. Once the ball is in motion on a horizontal surface, use the ruler to hit the ball as shown in the diagram. Describe the new motion of the ball and discuss what characteristics of the motion have been altered by the blow. Repeat with blows of various strengths.

   (b) Repeat (a) with balls of different sizes released from various initial heights on the ramp. Make a careful summary of your observations.

   (c) Release two balls simultaneously from the same height on the ramp but a few centimetres apart. When both balls are moving on a smooth flat surface, apply a sharp blow to one ball at 90° to its direction of motion, as shown above. Repeat the experiment several times. What happens to the ball that is hit? Explain your result.

The change in momentum of an object is a measure of the action exerted upon it. Newton called the action exerted on a body the '*vis impressa*'; we call it the **impulse**. In the next chapter, you will consider the concept of a force and the action of one particular force, the force of gravity.

Impulse, because it is a change in momentum, is a vector.

Example 3

A hockey ball of mass 0.5 kg is hit a glancing blow from a stick so that its velocity changes from $\begin{bmatrix} 6 \\ 8 \end{bmatrix}$ to $\begin{bmatrix} -9 \\ 7 \end{bmatrix}$ m s^{-1}, the axes being taken along and across the pitch. Find the ball's change in momentum in component form.

Solution

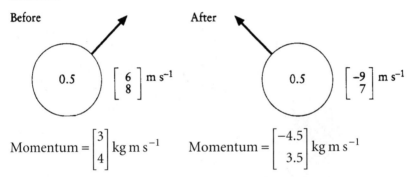

Before   After

$$\text{Momentum} = \begin{bmatrix} 3 \\ 4 \end{bmatrix} \text{kg m s}^{-1} \qquad \text{Momentum} = \begin{bmatrix} -4.5 \\ 3.5 \end{bmatrix} \text{kg m s}^{-1}$$

Change in momentum = Final momentum − Original momentum

$$= \begin{bmatrix} -4.5 \\ 3.5 \end{bmatrix} - \begin{bmatrix} 3 \\ 4 \end{bmatrix} = \begin{bmatrix} -7.5 \\ -0.5 \end{bmatrix} \text{kg m s}^{-1}$$

Exercise C (answers p. 142)

1   A 10 tonne truck is travelling along a straight road. Its speed increases from 65 km h^{-1} to 120 km h^{-1}. What is its change in momentum?

2   A railway truck on a straight track has a speed of 15 m s^{-1}. Its momentum decreases by 15 000 kg m s^{-1}. What is its new speed if the truck has:

(a) a mass of 2 tonnes   (b) a mass of 10 tonnes?

3 A puck of mass 0.1 kg is travelling across an ice rink with velocity $\begin{bmatrix} 25 \\ 2 \end{bmatrix}$ m s^{-1}. It is struck so that its new velocity is $\begin{bmatrix} -15 \\ 5 \end{bmatrix}$ m s^{-1}.

(a) What is the impulse?

(b) If the impulse had only been half this value, what would the new velocity have been?

After working through this chapter you should

1 know that the 'quantity of motion' of an object is called its momentum and that it is the product of the object's mass and velocity

2 know that a blow changes the momentum of an object in the direction of the blow

3 know that the change in momentum of a body due to a force is called the impulse

Change in momentum = $m\mathbf{v} - m\mathbf{u}$ = Impulse

4 know that momentum and impulse are vector quantities

5 know that total momentum is conserved if there are no external impulses

6 be able to use conservation of momentum to help determine the motion after a collision.

6 Force

A Newton's first and second laws of motion (answers p. 143)

Newton's first law of motion

In Chapter 5 you considered the fundamental 'quantity of motion' called momentum, and also studied changes in momentum.

To change the momentum of an object you must give it a push or a pull. The important features of a push or pull are its duration and its strength or **force**. For example, a tennis player applies a large force for a short period of time whereas a bowler in a game of cricket applies a smaller force for a longer period of time.

Without pushes or pulls the momentum of an object does not change. This important idea is called **Newton's first law of motion**.

> Unless acted upon by an external force, a particle travels with constant velocity (in a straight line with constant speed).

In 1673, some 14 years before Newton's *Principia*, Huygens expressed this idea as follows:

> If gravity did not exist, nor the atmosphere obstruct the motions of bodies, a body would maintain forever a motion once impressed upon it, with uniform velocity in a straight line.

It is important to note that Newton's first law states that the natural state of matter is motion with constant *velocity*. An object at rest is, of course, travelling with constant (zero) velocity!

The following two situations illustrate the application of Newton's first law.

Once a shot has left a shot-putter's hand it does not travel in a straight line with constant speed. If Newton's first law is to hold then there must be a force acting on the shot. That force is the pull of the Earth on the shot, i.e. its weight. This gradually changes the velocity of the shot.

Similarly, if you push a car along a level road, when you stop pushing it quickly comes to a halt. There must be a force acting on the car to bring it to rest. This force is **friction**. (It might not come to rest if it is on a slope, because then the weight of the car might overcome any frictional force.)

There are many forces, such as tension, weight, friction, and so on, which can act on an object. The **resultant force** is the combined effect of *all* forces acting on the object.

Newton's second law of motion

Newton realised that if the forces acting on an object are not balanced then the effect of the resultant force is to change the momentum of the object according to the law known as **Newton's second law of motion**. The questions which follow illustrate the ideas involved in the formulation of the very important second law.

1 A book slides across a table. The displacement x cm of the book at time t seconds is recorded in the table.

Distance travelled (x cm)	0	60	80	100	120
Time taken (t seconds)	0	0.7	1.0	1.4	2.0

(a) Plot the points and draw a graph showing distance travelled (vertical axis) against time (horizontal axis).

(b) As accurately as you can, draw tangents to the graph at $\frac{1}{2}$-second intervals to show that the speed of the book decreases at a constant rate of approximately 40 cm s^{-1} each second.

Since the mass of the book is constant, the constant rate of change of speed also means a constant rate of change of momentum. Newton recognised that rate of change of momentum is a measure of the resultant force being applied. In this case it indicates that there is a roughly constant frictional force acting on the book.

Newton's second law of motion states:

> **The resultant force on an object is equal to its rate of change of momentum** (its change of momentum each second).
>
> A force which causes a change in momentum of 1 kg m s^{-1} per second is said to be a force of 1 newton (1 N).

You may have already met an alternative version of Newton's second law where the resultant force is defined as the mass of the object multiplied by its 'acceleration'. This definition is consistent with the above version of the law and will be considered in Section C.

If the force acting is a constant force, then the change in momentum is simply the product of that force and the time over which it acts.

> A *constant* resultant force **F** acting on a body of mass m for a time t will cause a change in momentum of **F**t.
>
> Change in momentum = Resultant (constant) force × Time

Newton's first law arises as a special case of Newton's second law when the resultant force is zero.

In this case, the change in momentum is zero and therefore the momentum of the body remains constant.

$$m\mathbf{v} = \text{constant}$$

Provided the mass of the body is also constant, then the velocity (**v**) is constant.

Example 1

A constant force of 15 N is applied to a body of mass 10 kg for 5 seconds. If it starts from rest, what is its final velocity?

Solution

Change in momentum = force × time taken
$$= 5 \times 15 = 75 \text{ kg m s}^{-1}$$

Since the momentum is initially zero, the final momentum is 75 kg m s^{-1} and the final velocity is 7.5 m s^{-1} in the direction of the force.

Exercise A (answers p. 143)

1   A constant force of 20 N is applied for 4 seconds to a body of mass 2 kg, originally at rest. What is its speed after 1, 2, 3 and 4 seconds? What does this indicate about the motion of the body?

2   What force, acting for 5 seconds, would change the velocity of a puck of mass 0.2 kg from 1.5 m s^{-1} due south to 2 m s^{-1} due north?

3   How long does it take for the speed of a car, of mass 900 kg, to be reduced from 72 km h^{-1} to 48 km h^{-1} if the net braking force is 1250 N?

4   A train of mass 35 tonnes runs with a speed of 0.3 m s^{-1} into the buffers at the end of a platform. What constant force must the buffers exert to bring the train to rest in 2 seconds?

5   A hot air balloon of mass 200 kg rises up from the ground. If the resultant force on the balloon for the first 3 seconds is 150 N vertically upwards, what is its speed at the end of that time?

B Newton's third law (answers p. 143)

As we have seen, every mathematical model requires an initial set of assumptions. Newton's 'laws' are the basic assumptions on which the whole subject of mechanics depends. As well as the two we have introduced so far, there is one more.

Newton's third law states:

> When two bodies, A and B, interact, the force that A exerts on B is equal in magnitude and opposite in direction to the force that B exerts on A.

Among other things, this is the basis of conservation of momentum.

Consider the collision of two snooker balls. You can model the collision by supposing that two large reaction forces (**R** and **S**) act for a very short time.

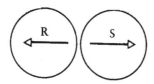

R and **S** are equal in magnitude and opposite in direction. Since they act for the same length of time, the changes in momentum must also be equal and opposite. So the total momentum of A and B before they make contact is equal to the total momentum after contact.

1D

Two students stand on skateboards and press against each other's hands. What can you say about:

(a) the force each exerts
(b) their subsequent motion?

If one student is twice as heavy as the other, how does this affect your answers to (a) and (b)?

Example 2

In deep space, a rocket changes its velocity by firing its engines. Explain how total momentum is conserved.

Solution

The rocket forces exhaust gases out of its motors in a given direction. These exert a force on the rocket which is equal in magnitude and opposite in direction to the force of the rocket on the gas.

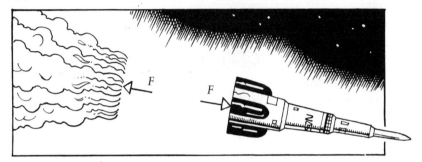

The change in momentum of the gas is therefore equal in magnitude and opposite in direction to the change in momentum of the rocket, and so the total momentum of the rocket and gas is conserved.

Exercise B (answers p. 144)

1   For a falling apple of weight W, what is the 'other body' which is involved? What is the other force? What can you say about the total momentum in the situation?

2   Draw a diagram and specify the forces of interaction involved in the motion of the Earth travelling round the Sun. Is the total momentum of the Earth and Sun constant? What does this tell you about the motion of the Sun?

C   Weight and change of momentum (answers p. 144)

This section considers the mechanics of objects falling freely in space and looks at the important concept of **weight**.

1D
(a) If a golf ball is allowed to fall freely, does the pull of the Earth change as it falls? Sketch the form of (time, velocity) graph you would expect.
(b) If a golf ball and cricket ball are dropped together (see p. 1) which will fall faster? Explain your answer.

Accurate data on falling objects can be obtained easily. Such data are studied in the following questions.

2 A 1 kg shot is dropped vertically from rest. From photographs of its motion, an accurate (time, displacement) graph has been drawn.

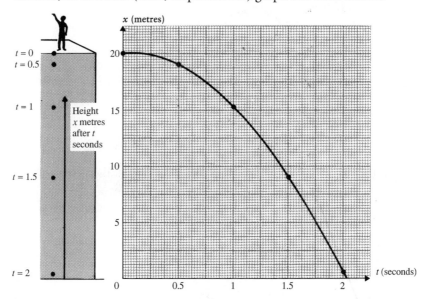

(a) From the (time, displacement) graph, estimate the velocity of the shot at half-second intervals. Hence draw the (time, velocity) graph.

(b) What is the change in momentum during:

    (i) the first second   (ii) the second second?

(c) If the shot were dropped from a much greater height, what do you think the change in momentum would be during the third second, the fourth second, and so on?

(d) What do you think causes this change in momentum?

3 The track of a golf ball as it is pitched onto the green is given below. It has been marked out every quarter second for the first six seconds of its flight.

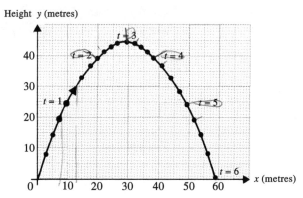

(a) To estimate the velocity of the ball one second after being hit, the displacement vector from $t = 0.75$ to $t = 1.25$ has been marked on the diagram. This is the displacement during a half second. A vector parallel to this but of twice the length therefore represents the average velocity during this time interval. This average velocity will be a good approximation to the velocity after one second.

Repeat this to find the velocity when $t = 2, 3, 4$ and 5 seconds.

(b) The mass of the ball is 0.1 kg. Find the five vectors representing the momenta of the ball 1, 2, 3, 4 and 5 seconds after being hit.

Draw them all with the same initial point:

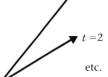

(c) What do you notice about these five vectors and what does this imply about the motion of the ball?

Find the changes in momentum of the ball during the second, third, fourth and fifth seconds of its flight.

(d) What do you notice about these changes in momentum? Try to explain what you find.

The force of gravitational attraction on an object is called the **weight** of the object. For an object which remains near the Earth's surface, this force is virtually constant. It is conventional to denote the weight of a 1 kg mass by the vector **g** newtons and its magnitude by g newtons. A sufficiently accurate value of g for most purposes is either 9.8 or 10.

Correspondingly, **g** is taken to be either $\begin{bmatrix} 0 \\ -9.8 \end{bmatrix}$ or $\begin{bmatrix} 0 \\ -10 \end{bmatrix}$

On a mass of m kg at the Earth's surface, the Earth exerts a downward force of $m\mathbf{g}$ newtons.

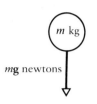

For an object moving freely under gravity (with negligible air resistance), the only force acting is its weight and it is easy to apply Newton's second law to its motion. For example, suppose a projectile has mass m kg and that during t seconds its velocity changes from $\mathbf{u}$ ms^{-1} to $\mathbf{v}$ ms^{-1}.

Original momentum + Time × Weight = New momentum

$$m\mathbf{u} \quad + \quad tm\mathbf{g} \quad = \quad m\mathbf{v}$$

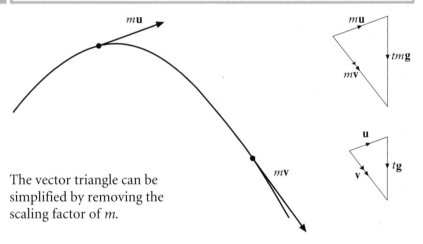

The vector triangle can be simplified by removing the scaling factor of m.

The velocity changes by $\mathbf{g}$ m s^{-1} each second. Another way of stating this is as follows.

A freely falling object has an acceleration downwards of $\mathbf{g}$ m s^{-2}.

Because of this result, $\mathbf{g}$ m s^{-2} is often called the **acceleration due to gravity**.

The relationship shown in the vector triangle can therefore be written as follows.

For an object moving freely under gravity,

Initial velocity + Time × Acceleration = Final velocity

$$\mathbf{u} \quad + \quad t\mathbf{g} \quad = \quad \mathbf{v}$$

A detailed study of acceleration and the corresponding form of Newton's second law,

$$\text{Resultant force} = \text{Mass} \times \text{Acceleration}$$

is given in the next three chapters.

Example 3

An apple is thrown vertically upwards at 20 m s^{-1}. What is its velocity after 4 seconds?

Draw a graph of velocity against time. When is its velocity zero?

Solution

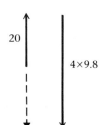

$$\mathbf{v} = \mathbf{u} + t\mathbf{g} = \begin{bmatrix} 0 \\ 20 \end{bmatrix} + 4 \times \begin{bmatrix} 0 \\ -9.8 \end{bmatrix}$$

The velocity (upwards) after 4 seconds is

$$20 - 4 \times 9.8 = -19.2 \text{ m s}^{-1}$$

From the graph you can see that the velocity is zero when $t \approx 2$.

The value from the graph can be confirmed as follows.

After t seconds, the upward velocity is

$$20 - t \times 9.8$$

This is zero when

$$t = \frac{20}{9.8} = 2.04 \quad \text{(to 3 s.f.)}$$

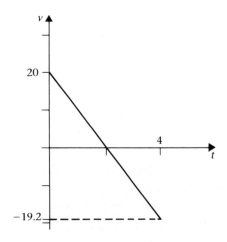

Example 4

A stone of mass 2 kg is dropped down a well. It hits the surface of the water 3 seconds later. How deep is the well?

Solution

Set up a model

Assume the stone is a particle (ignore its size).

Assume the only force acting on it is its weight, so its change of velocity is a constant 9.8 m s^{-1} each second.

Assume the stone starts from rest.

Analyse the problem

After 1 second its velocity is 9.8 m s^{-1}.

After 2 seconds its velocity is 19.6 m s^{-1}.

The (t, v) graph is as shown.

The shaded area under the graph gives the distance travelled as

$x = \frac{1}{2} \times 3 \times 29.4 = 44.1$ metres

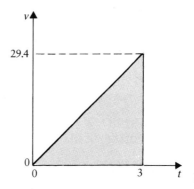

Interpret/validate

The stone travels about 44 metres so the well is at least 44 metres deep.

Exercise C (answers p. 145)

(Take $g = 9.8$ m s^{-2}.)

1 A ball rolls over a high cliff.
   (a) What is its velocity after 4 seconds?
   (b) How far has it fallen?
   (c) It hits the ground after 4.5 seconds. How high is the cliff?

2 A stone is thrown vertically upwards to dislodge a conker on a tree. The maximum speed the stone can be thrown with is 14.8 m s^{-1} and it must hit the conker with a speed of at least 5 m s^{-1} to dislodge it.
   (a) Draw a graph of velocity against time for the motion of the stone.
   (b) Use this to calculate the height of the highest conker it can dislodge.

3 A paint tin is dislodged from a workman's platform 4 metres above the street.
   (a) Draw a graph of velocity against time for the tin's motion.
   (b) Use your graph to calculate the velocity with which it hits the ground.

4 A girl of mass 25 kg and her father of mass 75 kg both jump off the 5 metre board into a swimming pool. What is the momentum of:

(a) the girl   (b) her father

when they reach the water?

5 A pile driver of mass 2 tonnes has a momentum of 16 000 kg m s^{-1} when it hits the ground. What height was it dropped from?

After working through this chapter you should

1 know Newton's three laws of motion
- unless acted upon by an external force, a particle travels with constant velocity
- resultant force equals rate of change of momentum
- when two bodies interact, they exert equal but opposite forces upon each other

2 know that a force of magnitude 1 newton gives a mass of 1 kg a change in velocity of 1 m s^{-1} each second

3 know that, on the Earth's surface, a mass of m kg has a weight of mg newtons, where $g \approx 9.8$

4 know the result that, for bodies moving freely under the gravitational attraction of the Earth,

$$\mathbf{v} = \mathbf{u} + t\mathbf{g}$$

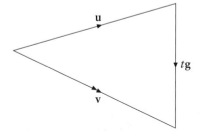

7 More kinematics

A Acceleration (answers p. 146)

1D What does the word 'acceleration' mean to the driver of a Formula 1 car?

What does acceleration mean to a mathematician?

Are the two ideas consistent?

So far you have only looked at the acceleration due to gravity. For this,

$$\mathbf{v} = \mathbf{u} + t\mathbf{g}$$

i.e. $\mathbf{g} = \dfrac{\mathbf{v} - \mathbf{u}}{t} = \dfrac{\text{change in velocity}}{\text{time}}.$

Whenever velocity changes at a steady rate, the change in velocity divided by the time is the (constant) acceleration. For motion always in the same direction, this is the rate of change of speed.

Example 1

A car on a straight motorway increases speed steadily from 50 km h^{-1} to 110 km h^{-1} in 20 seconds. Find its acceleration.

Solution

$$\text{Acceleration} = \frac{\text{change in velocity}}{\text{time}} = \frac{110 - 50}{20}$$
$$= 3 \text{ km h}^{-1} \text{ per second.}$$

Now 3 km h^{-1} per second $= 3000$ m h^{-1} per second
$$= \frac{3000}{3600} \text{ m s}^{-1} \text{ per second}$$
$$= 0.83 \text{ m s}^{-2}.$$

The first version of the answer is correct but unusual. The final answer is preferable.

A (velocity, time) graph is helpful, as we have seen, for questions about motion in a straight line.

2   Suppose that a body with acceleration a m s^{-2} changes velocity from u m s^{-1} to v m s^{-1} in t seconds, and travels s metres during this period:

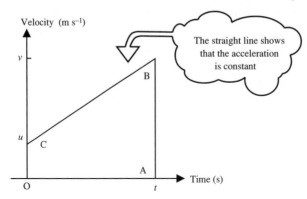

The straight line shows that the acceleration is constant

(a) Explain why the gradient of BC is a.

(b) Use the diagram to show that $v = u + at$.

(c) Show that $s = \frac{1}{2}(u + v)t$.

(d) Show that $s = ut + \frac{1}{2}at^2$

    (i) by combining the last two formulae
    (ii) direct from the (velocity, time) graph.

(e) Show that eliminating t from the first two formulae gives
$v^2 = u^2 + 2as$.

Note that the formula $s = \frac{1}{2}(u + v)t$ can be written in words as

    Displacement = Average velocity × Time.

The formulae apply just as well when some of the quantities are negative, as illustrated in the next example.

Example 2

A ball is thrown straight up with a speed of 12 m s^{-1}.

(a) Find its velocity and height after 2.1 seconds.

(b) Find the greatest height reached.

Solution

We take the upwards direction as positive and then the acceleration is -9.8 m s^{-2}.

(a) $u = 12$, $a = -9.8$, $t = 2.1$
    $v = u + at$ gives $v = 12 - 9.8 \times 2.1 = -8.58$
    $s = \frac{1}{2}(u + v)t$ gives $s = \frac{1}{2}(12 - 8.58) \times 2.1 = 3.59$.

(b) At the highest point, $v = 0$.
   $v^2 = u^2 + 2as$ gives $0 = 12^2 - 2 \times 9.8 \times s$, so $s = 7.35$.

Since g is only being taken to 2 s.f. and at every stage we have rounded values to 3 s.f., answers should only be given to 2 significant figures. The model gives the greatest height as 7.3 metres and after 2.1 seconds the ball is at height 3.6 metres and dropping at 8.6 metres per second.

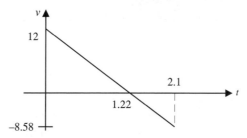

This example could have been solved straight from the (velocity, time) graph. The formulae just save a little time.

Exercise A (answers p. 146)

In each question, assume constant acceleration.

1   A car joins a motorway travelling at 14 $\overset{u}{m}$ s^{-1} and then accelerates at 0.8 m s^{-2} for 20 seconds. Find the distance travelled and the final speed.

2   A car accelerates from rest to 30 m s^{-1} (about 67 mph) in 12.6 seconds. Find the acceleration and the distance travelled.

3   A car brakes from 31 m s^{-1} to 10 m s^{-1} while travelling 250 m. Find the deceleration and the time taken to slow down.

4   A ball is thrown straight up with a speed of 5 m s^{-1} on the moon, where the acceleration due to gravity is 1.6 m s^{-2}. Find how high it rises and for how long it is 'in the air' before being caught at the same height from which it was thrown.

5   A ball is thrown straight up from the Earth's surface with a speed of 12 m s^{-1}. Find the speed when it is 5 m above the starting point and the two times at which it is at that height.

6   (a) A snooker ball hit at 1.8 m s^{-1} stops after travelling 3.2 m. Find the speed with which the ball would have hit a second ball 1.6 m from the starting point if it had been in the way.

   (d) A ball is struck at u m s^{-1} and stops in s metres. What was its velocity after going $\frac{1}{2}s$ metres?

B   Variable acceleration in straight line motion (answers p. 146)

When the (displacement, time) graph for motion in a straight line is a curve, the gradient $\dfrac{ds}{dt}$ represents the velocity. In the same way, the gradient of a (velocity, time) graph is the acceleration.

> Acceleration is the rate of change of velocity,
> $$a = \frac{dv}{dt}$$

Example 3

The motion of a particle along the x-axis is described by
$$x = t^3 - 6t^2 + 9t + 2$$
where x is in metres and the time t in seconds. Describe the motion.

Solution

By differentiation, $v = \dfrac{dx}{dt} = 3t^2 - 12t + 9 = 3(t^2 - 4t + 3)$
$$= 3(t-1)(t-3).$$

$$a = \frac{dv}{dt} = 6t - 12 = 6(t-2).$$

When $t = 0$, $x = 2$, $v = 9$, $a = -12$; so when the clock is started, the particle is 2 metres from the origin, travelling at 9 m s^{-1} away from the origin and slowing down at 12 m s^{-2}.

$v = 0$ when $t = 1$ and when $t = 3$;
$a = 0$ when $t = 2$.

The particle slows down until $t = 1$, at which time $x = 6$. For the next second, v and a are both negative; the particle is moving back towards the origin and speeding up. After 2 seconds, the acceleration is positive; the velocity goes from -3 m s^{-1} (when $t = 2$ and $x = 4$) to 0 m s^{-1} (when $t = 3$ and $x = 2$) and thereafter the particles moves in the x-direction at increasing speed.

The graph on the next page shows most of this information. Note that the line from (0, 10) to (2, 4) has gradient -3. Place a ruler along this line and verify that it is the tangent at (2, 4), confirming the maximum speed backwards.

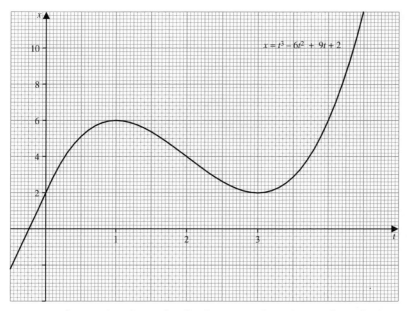

$$x = t^3 - 6t^2 + 9t + 2$$

In Example 3, going from the displacement function to the velocity function and on to the acceleration function involves two stages of differentiation. The reverse process, integration, is required to work back from acceleration to velocity and from velocity to displacement. Note that the constant terms in the expressions for x and v in Example 3 are the starting displacement and velocity.

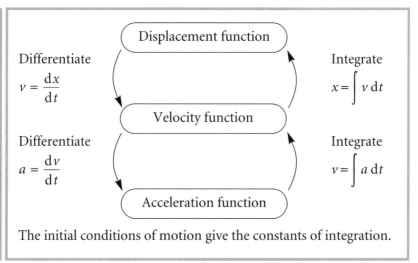

Differentiate

$v = \dfrac{dx}{dt}$

Displacement function

Integrate

$x = \displaystyle\int v\,dt$

Velocity function

Differentiate

$a = \dfrac{dv}{dt}$

Integrate

$v = \displaystyle\int a\,dt$

Acceleration function

The initial conditions of motion give the constants of integration.

1   A particle moves along the y-axis starting at $y = 2$ m and with velocity $3\ \mathrm{m\,s^{-1}}$. After t seconds, its acceleration $a\ \mathrm{m\,s^{-2}}$ is given by

$$a = t + 1.$$

Find its position, velocity and acceleration after 1 second.

Exercise B (answers p. 146)

In each question, a particle is moving along the x-axis. After t seconds, the displacement is x m, the velocity is v m s^{-1} and the acceleration is a m s^{-2}.

1   If $x = t^4 + t^2 + 3$, find v and a when $t = 2$.

2   If $a = t^2 - t + 1$, find v and x when $t = 1$ given that $v = 2$ and $x = 3$ when $t = 0$.

3   If $v = 3t^2 + 2t + 4$, find x and a in terms of t given that $x = 1$ when $t = 0$.

4   If a is always 10 and, when $t = 0$ then $x = 0$ and $v = 8$, find v and x as functions of t. Find the values of t and v when $x = 22$.

5   Show that two of the constant acceleration formulae can be obtained by integration starting from $\dfrac{\mathrm{d}v}{\mathrm{d}t} = a$.

C   Motion in two dimensions (answers p. 147)

A golf ball is chipped from just off the green. Its position at intervals of a fifth of a second has been marked on the graph below.

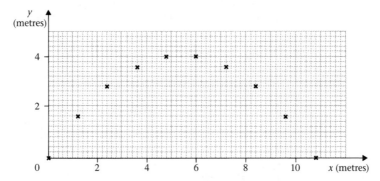

The position vectors are given in the table. (All distances are in metres.)

t	0.0	0.2	0.4	0.6	0.8	1.0	1.2	1.4	1.6	1.8
$\begin{bmatrix} x \\ y \end{bmatrix}$	$\begin{bmatrix} 0 \\ 0 \end{bmatrix}$	$\begin{bmatrix} 1.2 \\ 1.6 \end{bmatrix}$	$\begin{bmatrix} 2.4 \\ 2.8 \end{bmatrix}$	$\begin{bmatrix} 3.6 \\ 3.6 \end{bmatrix}$	$\begin{bmatrix} 4.8 \\ 4.0 \end{bmatrix}$	$\begin{bmatrix} 6.0 \\ 4.0 \end{bmatrix}$	$\begin{bmatrix} 7.2 \\ 3.6 \end{bmatrix}$	$\begin{bmatrix} 8.4 \\ 2.8 \end{bmatrix}$	$\begin{bmatrix} 9.6 \\ 1.6 \end{bmatrix}$	$\begin{bmatrix} 10.8 \\ 0 \end{bmatrix}$

To enable you to investigate the flight mathematically it is useful to first obtain a general expression for the position vector during the flight, t seconds after take-off.

1 Complete the formula for the position at time t.

$$\begin{bmatrix} x \\ y \end{bmatrix} = \begin{bmatrix} ? \\ 9t - 5t^2 \end{bmatrix}$$

Check that your formula fits the data given above.

If a particle is travelling in a straight line with constant velocity $\mathbf{v}$, then

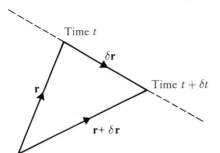

$$\mathbf{v} \approx \frac{\text{difference in position}}{\text{difference in time}} = \frac{\delta \mathbf{r}}{\delta t}$$

So in the limit as $\delta \mathbf{r}$ and $\delta t \rightarrow 0$,

$$\mathbf{v} = \frac{d\mathbf{r}}{dt}$$

Of course, the ball is *not* travelling in a straight line. However, if you magnify a small section of its flight path you will find that it is locally straight.

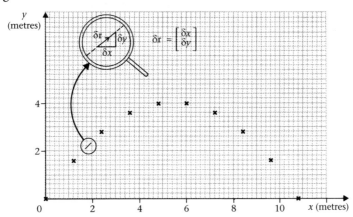

2 (a) Explain why $\mathbf{v} = \begin{bmatrix} \dfrac{dx}{dt} \\ \dfrac{dy}{dt} \end{bmatrix}$.

(b) Hence find $\mathbf{v}$ for $\mathbf{r} = \begin{bmatrix} 6t \\ 9t - 5t^2 \end{bmatrix}$.

(c) Calculate $\mathbf{v}$ when $t = 0.7, 0.9$ and 1.1 seconds.

(d) What is the speed of the ball when it lands?

(e) Interpret and validate your solutions.

The position vector **r** and velocity vector **v** of a projectile (or any other particle) are connected by the equation

$$\mathbf{v} = \frac{d\mathbf{r}}{dt}$$

$\dfrac{d\mathbf{r}}{dt}$ can be found by differentiating each component of **r**.

$$\frac{d\mathbf{r}}{dt} = \begin{bmatrix} \dfrac{dx}{dt} \\ \dfrac{dy}{dt} \end{bmatrix}$$

The velocity of the golf ball changes throughout the motion. For example, when $t = 0.4$, $\mathbf{v} = \begin{bmatrix} 6 \\ 5 \end{bmatrix}$ and when $t = 1.2$, $\mathbf{v} = \begin{bmatrix} 6 \\ -3 \end{bmatrix}$.

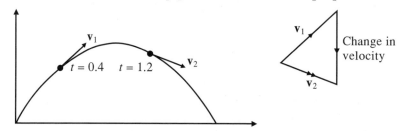

As you saw in Chapter 6, for motion under gravity the change in velocity each second is always constant at approximately 10 m s^{-1} downwards.

Here $\delta t = 1.2 - 0.4 = 0.8$, $\delta \mathbf{v} = \begin{bmatrix} 6 \\ -3 \end{bmatrix} - \begin{bmatrix} 6 \\ 5 \end{bmatrix} = \begin{bmatrix} 0 \\ -8 \end{bmatrix}$,

$$\frac{\delta \mathbf{v}}{\delta t} = \begin{bmatrix} 0 \\ -8 \end{bmatrix} \div 0.8 = \begin{bmatrix} 0 \\ -10 \end{bmatrix}.$$

For more general motion in two or three dimensions, the acceleration is defined as $\dfrac{d\mathbf{v}}{dt}$.

The velocity vector **v** and the acceleration vector **a** of a particle are connected by the equation

$$\mathbf{a} = \frac{d\mathbf{v}}{dt}.$$

$\frac{d\mathbf{v}}{dt}$ can be found by differentiating each component of **v**.

From $\mathbf{v} = \begin{bmatrix} 6 \\ 9 - 10t \end{bmatrix}$, note that differentiation gives $\mathbf{a} = \begin{bmatrix} 0 \\ -10 \end{bmatrix}$.

Example 4

The position vector of a golf ball, t seconds after being hit, is given by

$$\begin{bmatrix} x \\ y \end{bmatrix} = \begin{bmatrix} 10t \\ 30t - 5t^2 \end{bmatrix} \qquad \text{(All distances are in metres.)}$$

Find the golf ball's speed when it first strikes the ground (assumed to be horizontal).

Solution

It strikes the ground when $30t - 5t^2 = 0$
$$5t(6 - t) = 0$$
$$\implies \qquad t = 0 \text{ or } 6$$

Its velocity in m s^{-1} is given by $\mathbf{v} = \begin{bmatrix} 10 \\ 30 - 10t \end{bmatrix}$.

After 6 seconds, $\mathbf{v} = \begin{bmatrix} 10 \\ -30 \end{bmatrix}$ and its speed is $\sqrt{10^2 + 30^2} \approx 31.6 \text{ m s}^{-1}$.

Note that $\mathbf{a} = \dfrac{d\mathbf{v}}{dt} = \begin{bmatrix} 0 \\ -10 \end{bmatrix}$ as expected.

Exercise C (answers p. 147)

1 For the golf ball in Example 4 find
   (a) the time at which its velocity is horizontal
   (b) its maximum height
   (c) the horizontal distance it travels before it hits the ground.

2 Using the data for the ball given on page 80, what is the ball's speed
   (a) when it leaves the ground
   (b) when it is at the top of its flight?

3   Cannon-ball Kate is being fired out of a cannon into a safety net in a stunt to raise money for charity. Her position vector in metres is given by

$$\mathbf{r} = \begin{bmatrix} 20t \\ 11t - 5t^2 + 3 \end{bmatrix}$$

The landing net is 2 metres square and is placed at a height of 3 metres above the ground.

(a) Where should Kate's landing net be?

(b) What is her speed when she lands in the net?

4   The motion of a shot with position vector $\mathbf{r}$ metres at time t seconds is modelled by $\mathbf{r} = \begin{bmatrix} 10t \\ 2 + 10t - 5t^2 \end{bmatrix}$.

Calculate

(a) the magnitude and direction of the velocity of projection

(b) the height above ground level at which the shot was released by the shot-putter

(c) the distance of the throw

(d) the velocity of the shot on striking the ground

(e) when the velocity of the shot is horizontal

(f) the maximum height it attains above the ground.

5   The centre of gravity of a long-jumper, at time t seconds, has position vector

$$\mathbf{r} = \begin{bmatrix} 0.5 + 10t \\ 0.75 + 2.8t - 5t^2 \end{bmatrix} \text{metres}$$

where the origin is taken to be the take-off board.

(a) What is the initial or take-off velocity of the long-jumper?

(b) Where is her centre of gravity on take-off?

(c) Assume that on landing the centre of gravity is at the same height as on take-off. For how long is the jumper in the air and how long is the jump?

(d) Comment on the assumption made in this question.

6   Show that the acceleration is $\begin{bmatrix} 0 \\ -10 \end{bmatrix}$ m s^{-2} in each of questions 3, 4 and 5.

D Newton's second law, re-phrased (answers p. 148)

Newton expressed his second law in the form

Force = Rate of change of momentum.

1D Explain why Newton's second law can be written in the form
Force = Mass × Acceleration, i.e. $\mathbf{F} = m\mathbf{a}$.

It is important to note that $\mathbf{F} = m\mathbf{a}$ is a vector equation, so acceleration is a vector quantity and the acceleration vector and the force vector must act in the same direction. Any object will therefore accelerate in the direction of the resultant force acting on it. This is true even if the force is not constant.

For the model of the golf ball's motion in Section C, the only force is the weight giving the constant downward acceleration. To start with, this slows the ball down; later it speeds it up. All the time the ball is in the air, its path is curving.

Example 5

A 3 kg stone slides across the surface of a frozen lake in such a way that its position vector $\mathbf{r}$ metres at time t seconds is given by

$$\mathbf{r} = \begin{bmatrix} t^2 - 20t + 80 \\ -2t^2 + 40t \end{bmatrix} \qquad 0 \leqslant t \leqslant 10$$

Find the force acting on the stone. Show that this force is constant and acts in the opposite direction to the velocity of the stone.

Solution

By differentiating,

$$\frac{d\mathbf{r}}{dt} = \mathbf{v} = \begin{bmatrix} 2t - 20 \\ -4t + 40 \end{bmatrix}; \qquad \frac{d\mathbf{v}}{dt} = \mathbf{a} = \begin{bmatrix} 2 \\ -4 \end{bmatrix}$$

From Newton's second law, $\mathbf{F} = m\mathbf{a} = 3\begin{bmatrix} 2 \\ -4 \end{bmatrix} = 6\begin{bmatrix} 1 \\ -2 \end{bmatrix}$; therefore the

force is $\begin{bmatrix} 6 \\ -12 \end{bmatrix} = 6\begin{bmatrix} 1 \\ -2 \end{bmatrix}$ newtons.

The force is constant and parallel to the vector $\begin{bmatrix} 1 \\ -2 \end{bmatrix}$.

For $0 \leqslant t \leqslant 10$, $\mathbf{v} = (20 - 2t)\begin{bmatrix} -1 \\ 2 \end{bmatrix}$ is in the direction of the vector $\begin{bmatrix} -1 \\ 2 \end{bmatrix}$.

Hence $\mathbf{F}$ acts in the opposite direction to the motion of the stone and is presumably due to friction or air resistance.

Exercise D (answers p. 148)

1   An ice hockey puck is hit so that it has position vector

$$\mathbf{r} = \begin{bmatrix} 9t - t^2 \\ 9t - t^2 + 1 \end{bmatrix} \text{ metres for } 0 \leqslant t \leqslant 4.5 \text{ seconds.}$$

If the puck has mass 100 grams, find the force acting on the puck.

2   A skater's position on the ice is given by the position vector

$$\mathbf{r} = \begin{bmatrix} 5t - t^2 \\ 3 + 5t - t^2 \end{bmatrix} \text{ metres for } 0 \leqslant t \leqslant 2.5 \text{ seconds.}$$

Calculate the velocity and acceleration of the skater.

If the skater has mass 70 kg, calculate the force acting on him.

3   A child pulls a toy car along by means of a string, exerting a constant force on the string. If the position vector of the car, **r** metres at time t seconds, is given by $\mathbf{r} = \begin{bmatrix} 3t^2 \\ 4t^2 \end{bmatrix}$ and its mass is 500 grams, calculate the magnitude and direction of the pull exerted by the child.

4   A particle of mass 1.5 kg is at the origin when $t = 0$ and is travelling with velocity $\begin{bmatrix} 3 \\ 0 \end{bmatrix}$. It is acted on by a force $\begin{bmatrix} 0 \\ 3t \end{bmatrix}$. Find the acceleration vector, the velocity vector and the position vector.

Make a table to show the velocity and position vectors for values of $t = 0, 1, 2, 2.5$ and 3. Sketch the path of the particle, and show the velocity vectors on your sketch.

5   The movement of an object of mass 3 kg is affected by a force $\begin{bmatrix} -9t \\ 6 \end{bmatrix}$.

The object leaves the origin when $t = 0$ with velocity $\begin{bmatrix} 20 \\ 4 \end{bmatrix}$.

Find **v** and **r**, and sketch the path of the curve for the first 4 seconds. Draw vectors to show **v** and **a** at each second, checking that **v** is always a tangent to the curve, and **a** is always acting in a direction inwards from the curve.

6   A particle has velocity given by the vector $\begin{bmatrix} 6t^2 - 2t \\ 2t + 3 \end{bmatrix}$ where the units are m s^{-1}. Find the acceleration vector and the position vector given that initially $\mathbf{r} = \begin{bmatrix} 4 \\ -1 \end{bmatrix}$.

After working through this chapter you should

1   know and be able to apply the constant acceleration formulae for straight line motion

2   know that the velocity vector of a body is the rate of change of its position vector, and that the acceleration vector is the rate of change of velocity

$$\mathbf{v} = \frac{d\mathbf{r}}{dt}, \qquad \mathbf{a} = \frac{d\mathbf{v}}{dt}$$

3   know that the velocity vector can be found from the position vector by differentiation and the position vector from the velocity vector by integration

4   know that velocity and acceleration are connected similarly by differentiation and integration

5   know that Newton's second law of motion can be stated as

$$\mathbf{F} = m\mathbf{a}$$

(the acceleration is in the direction of the resultant force).

8 Projectile motion

A Motion under gravity (answers p. 149)

The motion of bodies that are thrown, dropped or launched into the air under the influence of gravity is called **projectile motion** if all other forces can be neglected. You can study this motion using vector equations for position, velocity and acceleration. We shall find that projectile motion always takes place in a vertical plane and the path is parabolic; the same shape as the graph of $y = x^2$. You can tell that the effects of air resistance and spin cannot be ignored when the path is clearly not parabolic or the motion is not in a vertical plane.

1D Give examples of projectile flight from sport and other daily life contexts. Also give examples where gravity cannot be taken as the only significant force.

For any projectile motion, the only force acting is taken to be weight, $\mathbf{W} = m\mathbf{g}$, acting downwards.

Taking axes horizontally and vertically upwards, $\mathbf{W} = \begin{bmatrix} 0 \\ -mg \end{bmatrix}$.

Hence Newton's second law, $\mathbf{F} = m\mathbf{a}$, gives $\mathbf{a} = \begin{bmatrix} 0 \\ -g \end{bmatrix}$.

In order to find out more about the velocity and position vector of a projectile, you will need to set up a model and analyse it. You can do this analysis in the problem which follows.

Problem

To find the highest point, the landing point and the flight time for an elastic band fired at a speed of 4.4 m s^{-1} at an angle of 30°.

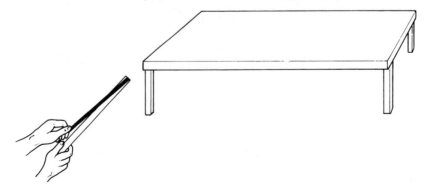

Set up a model

Assume the elastic band is a particle, projected from point A with a
speed of 4.4 m s^{-1} at 30° to the horizontal table AB. The elastic band
then flies for t seconds and lands R metres along the table at B.

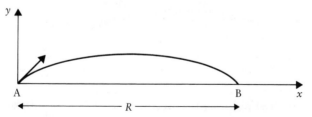

Choose x- and y-axes as shown, so that A has coordinates $(0, 0)$ and B
has coordinates $(R, 0)$. Assume that the elastic band of mass m has
constant weight mg, and take $g = 10$ m s^{-2}. What other assumptions
are made in this model?

Analyse the problem

The problem is to calculate R and t.

The acceleration is $\mathbf{a} = \begin{bmatrix} 0 \\ -g \end{bmatrix} = \begin{bmatrix} 0 \\ -10 \end{bmatrix}$ m s^{-2}.

You need to find the velocity $\mathbf{v}$ after any time t. Remember that if you
can differentiate $\mathbf{v}$ to obtain $\mathbf{a}$, you can integrate $\mathbf{a}$ to obtain $\mathbf{v}$.

$$\frac{d\mathbf{v}}{dt} = \begin{bmatrix} 0 \\ -10 \end{bmatrix}$$

Integrating, $\mathbf{v} = \begin{bmatrix} C_1 \\ -10t + C_2 \end{bmatrix}$ where C_1 and C_2 are constants.

The initial velocity is 4.4 m s^{-1} at an angle of 30° and so

$$\mathbf{v} = \begin{bmatrix} 4.4 \cos 30° \\ 4.4 \sin 30° \end{bmatrix} = \begin{bmatrix} 3.81 \\ 2.2 \end{bmatrix} \quad \text{when } t = 0$$

Therefore $\begin{bmatrix} C_1 \\ C_2 \end{bmatrix} = \begin{bmatrix} 3.81 \\ 2.2 \end{bmatrix}$ and $\mathbf{v} = \begin{bmatrix} 3.81 \\ 2.2 - 10t \end{bmatrix}$.

The horizontal component of velocity is a constant 3.81 m s^{-1}, but the
vertical component is decreasing at 10 m s^{-2}.

The band is at its highest point when $\mathbf{v} = \begin{bmatrix} 3.81 \\ 0 \end{bmatrix}$ m s^{-1}, i.e. when

$0 = 2.2 - 10t \Rightarrow t = 0.22$ seconds.

Answer questions 2 to 5 for the elastic band.

2 Integrate **v** to find the position vector **r** of the elastic band at time t. Check that you get the answers shown on the graph below.

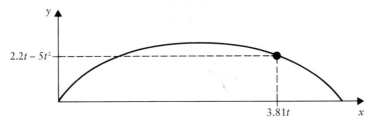

At the band's highest point $t = 0.22$ seconds, $y = 2.2t - 5t^2$ and so $y = 0.24$ metres.

Now consider the time, t, taken to land at B, where the y-coordinate is zero.

$$2.2t - 5t^2 = 0$$

3 (a) Solve the equation $2.2t - 5t^2 = 0$ to find t.

   (b) Use this value to find the range.

4 What are your conclusions?

5 You could validate your results experimentally. What difficulties and errors might arise?

Example 1

A girl puts a shot with velocity $\begin{bmatrix} 6 \\ 3.5 \end{bmatrix}$ m s^{-1}. If she releases it 1.5 metres above the ground, show that it hits the ground after 1 second. Find its speed of impact.

Solution

Assume that the shot is a particle of mass m kg and that air resistance can be neglected. Let the point of release be O and the point where it hits the ground be A.

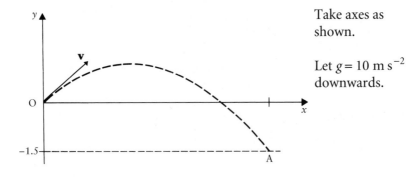

Take axes as shown.

Let $g = 10$ m s^{-2} downwards.

The force acting is $\begin{bmatrix} 0 \\ -mg \end{bmatrix}$ so the acceleration is $\dfrac{d\mathbf{v}}{dt} = \begin{bmatrix} 0 \\ -10 \end{bmatrix}$

By integration, $\mathbf{v} = \begin{bmatrix} 0 + c_1 \\ -10t + c_2 \end{bmatrix}$

When $t = 0$, $\mathbf{v} = \begin{bmatrix} 6 \\ 3.5 \end{bmatrix} \Rightarrow \mathbf{v} = \begin{bmatrix} 6 \\ 3.5 - 10t \end{bmatrix}$

Thus $\dfrac{d\mathbf{r}}{dt} = \begin{bmatrix} 6 \\ 3.5 - 10t \end{bmatrix} \Rightarrow \mathbf{r} = \begin{bmatrix} 6t + d_1 \\ 3.5t - 5t^2 + d_2 \end{bmatrix}$

When $t = 0$, $\mathbf{r} = \begin{bmatrix} 0 \\ 0 \end{bmatrix} \Rightarrow \mathbf{r} = \begin{bmatrix} 6t \\ 3.5t - 5t^2 \end{bmatrix}$

When $t = 1$, $\mathbf{r} = \begin{bmatrix} 6 \\ -1.5 \end{bmatrix}$

The shot hits the ground 6 metres away after 1 second.

When $t = 1$, $\mathbf{v} = \begin{bmatrix} 6 \\ -6.5 \end{bmatrix}$

The speed of impact is $\sqrt{36 + 42.25} = 8.8$ m s^{-1}.

Exercise A (answers p. 149)

In this exercise, ignore the effect of air resistance and take g to be 10 m s^{-2}.

1 Ann throws a ball to Julian with initial velocity $\begin{bmatrix} 7 \\ 5 \end{bmatrix}$ m s^{-1} and Julian catches it at the same height. For how long is the ball in the air? How far apart are Ann and Julian?

2 A high-jumper takes off with initial velocity $\begin{bmatrix} 3 \\ 5 \end{bmatrix}$ m s^{-1}.

At take-off her centre of gravity is approximately 1 metre above the ground. Write down the velocity and position vector of her centre of gravity at time t seconds after take-off.

What is the maximum height of her centre of gravity?

3 A discus is projected at an angle of 40° with a speed of 21 m s^{-1} and from a height above the ground of 2 metres.

Calculate its velocity and position vector at time t. What is the length of the throw?

4E

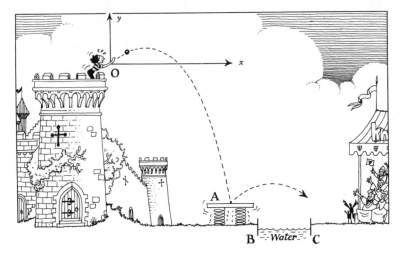

The picture shows a contestant in a TV game show standing on top of a tower. She hurls a cannon-ball of mass 8 kg from point O. Her objective is to make the cannon-ball bounce on a smooth horizontal platform at A, and then rebound across the water hazard BC. Taking axes through O as shown and with units of metres, A is the point $(8, -10)$ and C is $(11, -12)$.

(a) If the initial velocity is $\begin{bmatrix} 4 \\ 5 \end{bmatrix}$ m s^{-1} show that the cannon-ball

will land at A when two seconds have elapsed, with

velocity $\begin{bmatrix} 4 \\ -15 \end{bmatrix}$ m s^{-1}.

(b) Assuming that momentum is conserved in the collision between the cannon-ball and the sprung platform (which can be modelled as a heavy, smooth rigid block of mass 48 kg, and which acquires

a velocity $\begin{bmatrix} 0 \\ -3 \end{bmatrix}$ m s^{-1} immediately after impact), show that

the initial velocity of the cannon-ball as it bounces off the

block is $\begin{bmatrix} 4 \\ 3 \end{bmatrix}$ m s^{-1}.

(c) Does the cannon-ball clear the water hazard?

5E A missile leaves a plane at a height of 3000 m and moves so that t seconds later its displacement **r** in metres is given by

$$\mathbf{r} = \begin{bmatrix} 3t \\ 4t \\ -5t^2 \end{bmatrix}$$

with respect to axes in the directions south, east and vertically upwards respectively.

(a) Find its velocity after t seconds.

(b) Show that initially the missile is travelling horizontally, and calculate its bearing.

(c) Show that its speed after 2 seconds is $5\sqrt{17}$ m s^{-1}.

(d) Calculate the missile's distance from its starting point after 2 seconds.

(e) Find when it hits the ground.

(f) Calculate its acceleration and hence state, with a brief reason, whether it is powered or not.

B The general case (answers p. 150)

For a more general case of projectile motion, you could take axes to be horizontal (x) and vertical (y) such that, at $t = 0$, the projectile has position vector $\begin{bmatrix} a \\ b \end{bmatrix}$ and initial velocity $\begin{bmatrix} u_x \\ u_y \end{bmatrix}$.

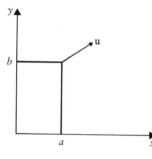

Assume that the only force acting is gravity.

So $\mathbf{a} = \dfrac{d\mathbf{v}}{dt} = \begin{bmatrix} 0 \\ -g \end{bmatrix}$ and, integrating this,

$\mathbf{v} = \begin{bmatrix} u_x \\ -gt + u_y \end{bmatrix}$ since $\mathbf{v} = \begin{bmatrix} u_x \\ u_y \end{bmatrix}$ when $t = 0$.

Since $\mathbf{v} = \dfrac{d\mathbf{r}}{dt}$, direct integration gives

$\mathbf{r} = \begin{bmatrix} u_x t + a \\ -\frac{1}{2}gt^2 + u_y t + b \end{bmatrix}$

since $\mathbf{r} = \begin{bmatrix} a \\ b \end{bmatrix}$ when $t = 0$.

Often, projectile motion assumes projection from the origin with velocity of magnitude u at an angle ϕ to the horizontal.

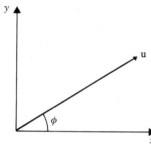

So $u_x = u \cos \phi$

$u_y = u \sin \phi$

and a and b are zero.

This gives $\mathbf{v} = \begin{bmatrix} u \cos \phi \\ -gt + u \sin \phi \end{bmatrix}$ and $\mathbf{r} = \begin{bmatrix} ut \cos \phi \\ -\frac{1}{2}gt^2 + ut \sin \phi \end{bmatrix}$.

Exercise B (answers p. 150)

For question 5 onwards take g as 10 m s^{-2} unless stated otherwise. Ignore air resistance.

1 (a) When $t = \dfrac{2u \sin \phi}{g}$, calculate **r**.

   (b) Interpret your result. How can it be validated?

2 (a) At the highest point on the path of a projectile, the vertical component of the velocity is zero. Use this fact to find an expression, in terms of u, g and ϕ, for the time taken to reach the highest point.

   (b) Use this result to show that the height reached is $\dfrac{u^2 \sin^2 \phi}{2g}$.

   (c) Interpret this result as u and ϕ vary. Validate it practically in a suitable experiment.

3 Show that for a projectile starting from the origin with initial velocity **U**

   $$\mathbf{v} = \mathbf{U} + \mathbf{g}t$$
   $$\mathbf{r} = \mathbf{U}t + \tfrac{1}{2}\mathbf{g}t^2$$

4 Show that the result of eliminating t from the equations

   $$x = Ut \cos \phi$$
   $$y = Ut \sin \phi - \tfrac{1}{2}gt^2$$

   is an equation of the form $y = -px^2 + qx$, showing that the path is a parabola. Express p and q in terms of U, ϕ and g.

5 At a given instant, a group of objects is projected horizontally from the edge of a table. Each object has a different initial speed.

   What can you say about the motion of each object as time increases?

6 A golf ball is hit so that it leaves the ground with initial velocity of magnitude 25 m s^{-1}, at an angle α, where $\tan \alpha = \tfrac{4}{3}$, as shown in the diagram.

   (a) How high does the ball go?
   (b) How far does it travel before its first bounce if the ground is horizontal?

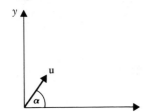

7 Two children throw stones into the sea. Jill throws her stone at an angle of 60° to the horizontal and speed 20 m s^{-1}, while Jack throws his stone at a 40° angle and can only manage an initial speed of 15 m s^{-1}. Both stones are thrown simultaneously and both are released at a height 1.4 m above sea level.

(a) How high does Jill throw her stone?

(b) Which stone lands in the water first?

(c) Whose stone lands further away?

8 A small relief plane is flying horizontally at 30 m s^{-1}. Its height is 210 m. A package, released from the plane, just clears some trees which are 30 m high.

(a) At what horizontal distance from the trees is the package released?

(b) How far beyond the trees does the package land?

9 Ahmed throws a ball to Susan who is 80 m away and who catches it at the same height as it was thrown. The ball is in the air for 5 seconds. Taking the acceleration g as 9.8 m s^{-2}, find the initial velocity of the ball.

10 At what angle should a projectile be launched if it is to achieve the maximum possible horizontal range?

Find out the greatest recorded distance a cricket ball has ever been thrown. Estimate the initial speed of the ball.

11 A rugby player takes a penalty kick. He places the ball at a point O on the ground, 12 metres away from the goal line and directly in front of the goal, and he kicks it at a right angle to the goal line at an angle of 40° to the horizontal. The ball passes over the crossbar at point P, 4 metres above the ground. Estimate the initial speed of the ball.

After working through this chapter you should

1 know that in projectile motion, the only force is assumed to be weight, acting vertically downwards

2 know how to model projectile motion in a variety of problems and situations

3 for projection from the origin

$$\mathbf{a} = \frac{d\mathbf{v}}{dt} = \begin{bmatrix} 0 \\ -g \end{bmatrix}$$

$$\mathbf{v} = \frac{d\mathbf{r}}{dt} = \begin{bmatrix} u\cos\theta \\ -gt + u\sin\theta \end{bmatrix}$$

$$\mathbf{r} = \begin{bmatrix} ut\cos\theta \\ -\frac{1}{2}gt^2 + ut\sin\theta \end{bmatrix}$$

9 Force and motion

A Contact forces (answers p. 152)

You have seen that:

- Unless acted upon by an external force, a particle travels with constant velocity.
- The resultant force on an object is equal to its rate of change of momentum, which is equal to mass times acceleration.

    $\mathbf{F} = m\mathbf{a}$

- When two bodies interact, they exert equal but opposite forces upon each other.

One type of pushing force with which you will be very familiar is that of a contact force between surfaces.

If a box rests on a table, then the box pushes against the table and the table pushes against the box. $\mathbf{R}$ is the total contact force on the box from the table. In this case, Newton's third law of motion says that there is an equal but opposite force acting on the table.

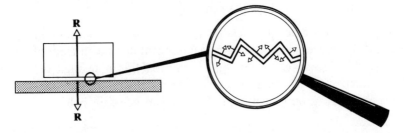

You can model the situation with a large number of 'contact forces'. Note that the sum of all the contact forces on the box gives the total contact force. This is conventionally modelled as a single force.

The most useful force diagram to draw is usually one showing *all* the forces acting on one object. For a box on a table you might draw:

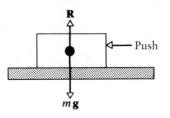

There is no acceleration vertically, and so by Newton's first law

$$\mathbf{R} = -m\mathbf{g}$$

in vector form or, considering only magnitudes,

$$R = mg.$$

Even when the box is on a slope, if it does not move then the contact force is vertically upwards to maintain the equilibrium and again $\mathbf{R} = -m\mathbf{g}$. Note that $\mathbf{R}$ is not perpendicular to the surface.

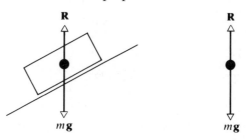

Objects are modelled as particles. This is done by drawing a dot in the object and showing *all* the forces acting on the dot, as shown above.

It is sometimes convenient to consider the contact force as a combination of two forces, a **normal contact force** perpendicular to the surface and a force called **friction** which acts parallel to the surfaces in such a direction as to oppose any tendency to slide.

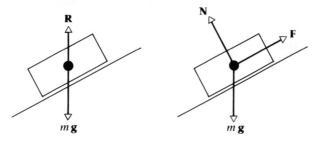

$\mathbf{N}$ and $\mathbf{F}$ are called components of the contact force $\mathbf{R}$. This idea is studied further in Section C. It is important to note that you can use either $\mathbf{R}$ or its components but *not both* on the same diagram.

If a box is pushed across a rough horizontal surface, friction opposes the motion and the force diagram is:

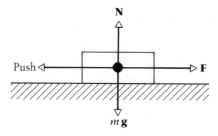

If the box does not move then there is no change in momentum. The resultant force on the box is therefore zero. The normal contact force is balanced by the weight and the push is balanced by the friction force.

The normal contact force and the frictional force may be represented by a single contact force, **R**. The force diagram for this is:

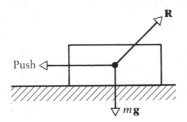

In the illustration, a loaded sledge is being pulled up a slight incline.

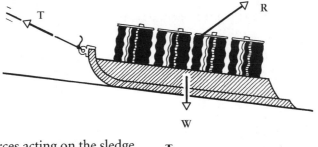

The forces acting on the sledge can be modelled by the force diagram shown.

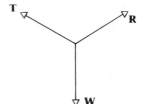

There are three forces – the pull of the rope on the sledge, the weight of the sledge and the contact force between the slope and the sledge. This last force (**R**) is split into a normal contact force **N** and a frictional force **F** in the figure below.

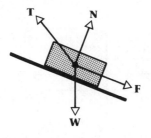

The contact force, **R**, of one object on another may be replaced by a normal contact force, **N**, perpendicular to the surface, and a friction force, **F**, parallel to the surface which acts to oppose motion. This friction force may, of course, be zero.

Exercise A (answers p. 152)

1 The six diagrams provide models of the forces acting on various objects. For each, give a possible description of the forces.

(a)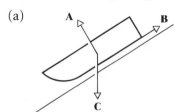

A sledge sliding down a slope

(b)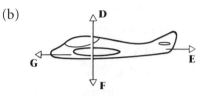

An aeroplane in flight

(c)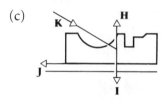

A toy being pushed across a floor by a child leaning over it

(d)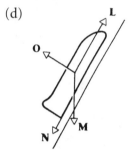

An injured climber being pulled up an ice face

(e)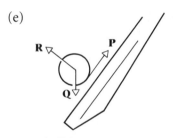

A ball being struck with a bat

(f)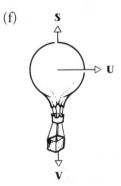

A hot-air balloon ascending and being blown by a side wind

2 Draw a force diagram for the injured climber of question 1(d) if she is being winched *down* the ice face.

3 Draw a force diagram for a toy being pulled across the floor by a string
  (a) if the contact force between the floor and the toy is shown as a single force
  (b) if the contact force is divided into its two components.

4 For each of the following situations draw a diagram to model the forces you think are appropriate. Consider the object in bold type:

(a) a **girl** sliding downhill on a toboggan

(b) the **toboggan** in part (a)

(c) a **car** being given a push start by a man

(d) the **man** in part (c)

(e) a **ship** at anchor

(f) a **ski-jumper** when she is in the air

(g) a **ski-diver** in mid-air falling straight down.

B Adding forces (answers p. 153)

1D

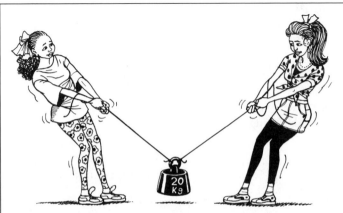

The picture shows two girls using ropes to hold a heavy object just above the ground.

Describe what happens to the pull from the ropes if the girls are standing

(a) close together

(b) one metre apart

(c) four metres apart.

Try this practically using a heavy school-bag and some string. Can you lift the bag high enough so that the strings are horizontal? Explain your answer.

You know that forces are vectors. This implies that they can be added in just the same way as displacements and velocities.

The combined effect of a number of forces, the **resultant** force, can be found

  (i) by using components,

  (ii) by drawing,

or (iii) by sketching the vector diagram then using trigonometry.

Example 1

Find the resultant of two forces, 5 newtons and 7 newtons, which contain an angle of 70°.

Solution

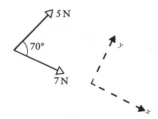

Method 1

With x and y directions as shown,

$$\mathbf{R} = \begin{bmatrix} 7 \\ 0 \end{bmatrix} + \begin{bmatrix} 5\cos 70° \\ 5\sin 70° \end{bmatrix} = \begin{bmatrix} 8.71 \\ 4.70 \end{bmatrix}$$

$$\sqrt{8.71^2 + 4.70^2} = 9.9, \qquad \tan^{-1}\left(\frac{4.70}{8.71}\right) = 28°$$

The resultant is a force of 9.9 N at 28° to the 7 N force.

Method 2

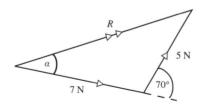

R and α can be measured from the scale diagram.

Method 3

$$R^2 = 7^2 + 5^2 - 2 \times 7 \times 5 \times \cos 110°$$
$$R = 9.90$$

$$\sin \alpha = \frac{5\sin 110°}{R} \implies \alpha = 28.3°$$

Method 1 is usually the best, especially when there are three or more forces.

If a body is either at rest or moving with constant velocity, its acceleration is zero. The vector sum of the forces acting on the body is zero and hence the forces form a closed polygon.

Example 2

The four forces shown acting on a particle are in equilibrium. Find the magnitude and direction of **P**.

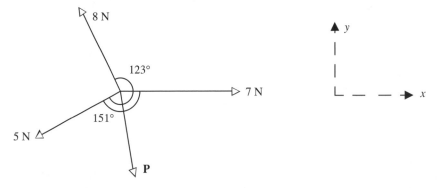

Solution

The resultant force is zero.

Take x and y directions as shown.

$$\begin{bmatrix} 7 \\ 0 \end{bmatrix} + \begin{bmatrix} 8 \cos 123° \\ 8 \sin 123° \end{bmatrix} + \begin{bmatrix} 5 \cos(-151°) \\ 5 \sin(-151°) \end{bmatrix} + \mathbf{P} = \begin{bmatrix} 0 \\ 0 \end{bmatrix}$$

$$\begin{bmatrix} 7 \\ 0 \end{bmatrix} + \begin{bmatrix} -4.36 \\ 6.71 \end{bmatrix} + \begin{bmatrix} -4.37 \\ -2.42 \end{bmatrix} + \mathbf{P} = \begin{bmatrix} 0 \\ 0 \end{bmatrix}$$

$$\mathbf{P} = \begin{bmatrix} 1.73 \\ -4.29 \end{bmatrix}$$

or 4.6 N at 68° below the x-direction.

2 The photographs on pages 103 and 104 show some experiments to validate the following statements.

(a) The resultant of two forces can be found by adding the forces as vectors.

(b) If a particle is in equilibrium then the vector sum of the forces acting on it is zero.

(c) Three or more forces can be added by drawing a vector polygon.

Carry out your own experiments to validate one or more of the above. Your class could split into groups, with each group reporting back to the whole class and giving a clear description of their experiment and the conclusions they have reached. You may want to use some of the ideas shown or design your own experiment.

Using a rubber band

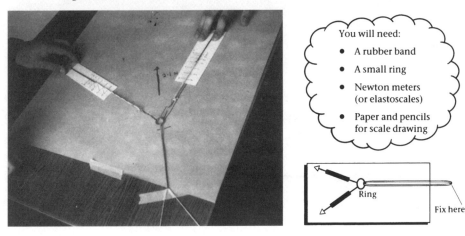

You will need:
- A rubber band
- A small ring
- Newton meters (or elastoscales)
- Paper and pencils for scale drawing

Ring

Fix here

Hints

- Loop one end of the rubber band around the ring and fix the other end to the table.
- Hook a couple of newton meters in the ring and use them to stretch the rubber band to a certain length.
- Draw line vectors on the paper to model, in magnitude and direction, the pulls of the newton meters on the ring.
- Now use a single newton meter to extend the rubber band to the same point.
- Draw a line vector representing the pull of the single newton meter on the ring.

What can you say about the three force vectors you have drawn?

Using pulleys and masses

You will need

• two pulleys

• three sets of masses

• string

Hints

● Tie three pieces of string together in a knot at A and put loops in the other ends of the strings.

● Suspend the masses on the pulleys in front of a sheet of paper as shown.

● Draw line vectors on the paper to model the forces acting on the knot at A.

What can you say about the three force vectors you have drawn?

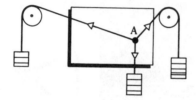

Using pieces of string

You will need

• string

• newton meters

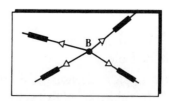

Hints

● Tie four pieces of string together in a knot B. Put loops in their other ends.

● Hook a newton meter in each loop and pull them tight on a sheet of paper.

● Draw line vectors on the paper to model, in magnitude and direction, the pull of each of the newton meters on the knot B.

What can you say about the four force vectors you have drawn?

Exercise B (answers p. 154)

1 Find the resultants of the pairs of forces shown in the diagrams.

(a)

4 N

5 N

(b)

1.5 N

120°

0.8 N

2 Gillian and Paul give Zia's car a push start. Gillian pushes straight ahead with a force of 420 N. Paul pushes with a force of 500 N at an angle of 25° to the line of the car. Calculate the magnitude and the direction of the resultant of these two pushes.

3 Two tugs are towing a large ship into harbour, pulling on the bows of the ship with horizontal cables. The far tug is pulling with a force of 52 000 N at an angle of 23° to the forward motion of the ship and the near tug pulls with a force of 68 000 N at an angle of 18° to the motion. Calculate the resultant pull on the ship.

4 The frictional force between an object and the ground is 80 N. If the normal contact force is 200 N then calculate the magnitude and direction of the total contact force.

5 Two forces of magnitude 3 N and 4 N have a resultant of magnitude 6 N. Find the angle between the two forces.

6 The following groups of forces are in equilibrium. Find the magnitude and direction of the forces labelled by letters.

(a)

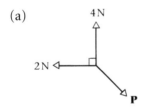

4 N

2 N

P

(b)

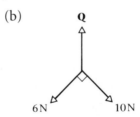

Q

6 N   10 N

(c)

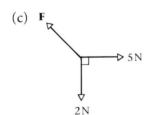

F

5 N

2 N

(d)

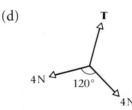

T

4 N

120°

4 N

7 A shopping bag of mass 15 kg is carried by two people. If they walk so that their arms make an angle of 50° with the horizontal, what force must each of them exert on the bag? Estimate the likely minimum angle at which they can hold the bag.

C Resolving forces (answers p. 155)

You know that the total contact force **R** may be considered as the sum of a frictional force **F** and a normal contact force **N**.

Splitting a force into components at right angles to each other is called **resolving**.

In general, any force **F** can be resolved into two perpendicular components $F \cos \phi$ and $F \sin \phi$ acting in the directions shown.

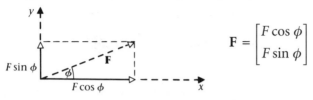

$$\mathbf{F} = \begin{bmatrix} F \cos \phi \\ F \sin \phi \end{bmatrix}$$

You can choose any directions you like for your x- and y-axes. Sometimes one choice turns out to be more convenient than another.

Example 3

Repeat Example 1 with a different choice of axes.

Solution

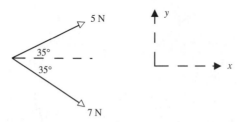

With these axes,

$$\mathbf{R} = \begin{bmatrix} 5 \cos 35° \\ 5 \sin 35° \end{bmatrix} + \begin{bmatrix} 7 \cos 35° \\ -7 \sin 35° \end{bmatrix} = \begin{bmatrix} 12 \cos 35° \\ -2 \sin 35° \end{bmatrix} = \begin{bmatrix} 9.83 \\ -1.15 \end{bmatrix}$$

Now $\sqrt{9.83^2 + 1.15^2} = 9.9,$ $\tan^{-1}\left(\dfrac{-1.15}{9.83}\right) = -6.7°.$

These agree with the answers found earlier.

Exercise C (answers p. 155)

1   The force **F** is of magnitude 50 newtons at 30° to the horizontal. In each of the following cases resolve **F** into its components

(a) horizontally and vertically

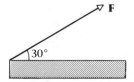

(b) up the slope and perpendicular to the slope

(c) down the slope and perpendicular to the slope.

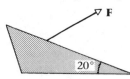

2   Resolve the following forces into perpendicular components in the directions indicated.

(a)

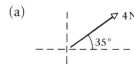

(b)

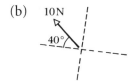

(c)

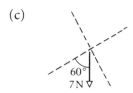

(d)

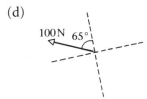

3

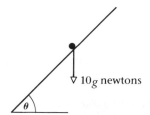

A mass of 10 kg is resting on a rough inclined plane as shown.

(a) Draw a force diagram and, by considering components parallel to the plane, calculate the magnitude of the force of friction, F, if $\theta = 20°$.

(b) If N is the magnitude of the normal contact force, show that

$$\frac{F}{N} = \tan \theta$$

4   By resolving one or both forces into components, calculate the resultant of the forces 11 N and 9 N shown in the diagram.

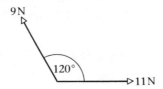

5   By resolving each force into components, find the resultant of the following sets of forces.

(a)

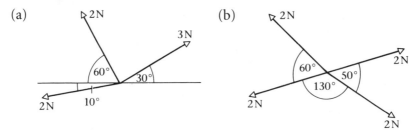

(b)

6   Three children each think that a parcel has stopped at them in a game of 'pass the parcel'. They pull on parts of the parcel with forces of 20 N, 40 N and 35 N at angles of 120°, 150° and 90° with each other as shown in the diagram.

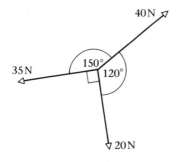

If the parcel does not break, in which direction will it move?

7   The diagram on the next page shows a boy held (at rest) by two ropes. The mass of the boy is 60 kg. Find the tension in each of the ropes
    (a) by taking components horizontally and vertically
    (b) by taking components parallel and perpendicular to one of the ropes.

8 Two masses of *m* grams each are suspended over two friction-free pulleys. A mass of 60 grams is hung between them as shown. If the strings both make an angle of 45° to the vertical, find *m*.

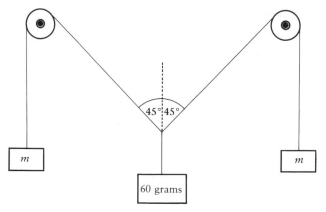

9 A mass of 20 kg is supported by two strings inclined to the vertical at 30° and 60°. Calculate the tension in each string.

D Force and acceleration (answers p. 156)

The following diagram was obtained earlier (p. 98), when modelling a sledge (of mass 750 kg) being pulled up a slope.

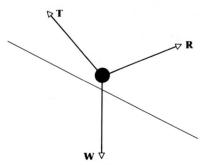

The values for some of the angles and forces have been included on the diagram below. The total contact force is split into a normal contact force and a friction force of 250 N.

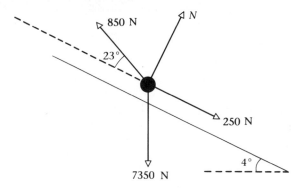

The weight of the sledge is $750 \times 9.8 = 7350$ N .

1D   Finding N is quite easy if you make a good choice of directions in which to resolve the forces. What directions would you choose?

Find N and also find the resultant force on the sledge.

What is the acceleration of the sledge?

The choice of directions in which to resolve the forces can be critical for finding straightforward solutions to problems.

Example 4

A book of mass 3 kg is placed on a smooth slope of angle 25°. It starts to slide down the slope. What is the contact force on the book? What is its acceleration? (Take $g = 10$ ms^{-2}.)

Solution

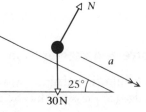

The slope is smooth so the contact force is normal to the slope. The acceleration is a m s^{-2} down the slope. Taking axes along and perpendicular to the slope,

by Newton's second law $\begin{bmatrix} 30 \sin 25° \\ N - 30 \cos 25° \end{bmatrix} = 3 \begin{bmatrix} a \\ 0 \end{bmatrix}$

$$30 \sin 25° = 3a \quad \Rightarrow \quad a = 4.23$$

$$\text{and } N - 30 \cos 25° = 0 \quad \Rightarrow \quad N = 27.2$$

The contact force is 27.2 newtons at right angles to the slope (to 3 s.f.). The book accelerates down the slope at 4.23 m s^{-2} (to 3 s.f.).

Exercise D (answers p. 157)

(Take $g = 10$ ms^{-2}.)

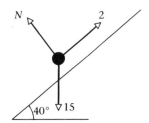

1 A block is sliding down a slope. The forces acting on it are shown in the diagram (in newtons). Find the normal contact force N newtons. What is the acceleration of the block?

2 A trolley of mass 200 kg is being pulled up a smooth slope of 20° by a rope parallel to the slope. If the tension in the rope is 800 newtons, find the acceleration of the trolley.

3 A girl of mass 65 kg is abseiling down a rope fixed to the top of a cliff. If the tension in the rope is 540 newtons, what is the resultant force on the girl? Find her acceleration. What happens if the rope breaks?

4 A ball of mass 1 kg is falling through the air with an acceleration of 6 m s^{-2}. Calculate the air resistance.

5 A woman weighing 60 kg is standing in a lift. What is the magnitude of the contact force between her and the lift if the lift is moving

(a) upwards with constant speed

(b) upwards with acceleration 1.5 m s^{-2}

(c) downwards with acceleration 1.5 m s^{-2}?

E Model of static friction (answers p. 157)

1D A man is trying to push a heavy crate across a warehouse floor. It is too hard to move so more and more people come to help. It finally moves when there are 5 people pushing. Discuss the friction force between the crate and the floor. Is it constant the whole time? What might it depend on? Set up a class experiment, as shown, to find out how static friction, F newtons, depends on the normal contact force, N newtons.

The experiment with the block in question 1D above will have shown that the maximum friction force (equal to the force just required to make the block move) is roughly proportional to the normal reaction (equal in this case to the weight of the block plus any extra load). The constant of proportion is called the coefficient of friction and denoted by μ.

Static friction

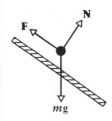

Friction acts in a direction along the surface of contact to prevent motion.

$$F \leqslant \mu_S N$$

where μ_S is the coefficient of static friction, which depends upon the nature of both surfaces.

Typical values and ranges of values of μ_S are indicated in the table.

Surfaces in contact	μ_S
Wood against wood	0.2–0.5
Wood against metal	0.2–0.6
Metal against metal	0.15–0.3
Plastic against rubber	0.7
Sandpaper against sandpaper	2.0
Metal on snow	0.02

Example 5

A box is placed on a rough plane which is gradually tilted. The box is on the point of sliding when the plane makes an angle of α to the horizontal. Find the coefficient of static friction between the box and the plane.

Solution

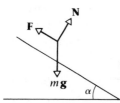

Let the friction force be F newtons and the normal contact force be N newtons, as shown. The forces are in equilibrium. Using Newton's second law,

$$\mathbf{F} + \mathbf{N} + m\mathbf{g} = 0$$

$$\begin{bmatrix} F \\ 0 \end{bmatrix} + \begin{bmatrix} 0 \\ N \end{bmatrix} + \begin{bmatrix} -mg \sin \alpha \\ -mg \cos \alpha \end{bmatrix} = \begin{bmatrix} 0 \\ 0 \end{bmatrix}$$

$\Rightarrow \quad F = mg \sin \alpha \quad$ and $\quad N = mg \cos \alpha$

But $F = \mu N$ as the box is about to slide

so $mg \sin \alpha = \mu mg \cos \alpha$

$\Rightarrow \quad \mu = \tan \alpha$

Exercise E (answers p. 157)

Take $F \leqslant \mu_S N$ for your model of static friction and $g = 10 \text{ m s}^{-2}$.

1 A crate of weight 100 newtons rests on a rough plane inclined at 30° to the horizontal. It is just about to slip.

(a) What is the force due to friction on the crate?

(b) Find the coefficient of static friction between the crate and the plane.

2 A rubber of mass m kilograms is placed on a table. The coefficient of static friction between the two surfaces is 0.7. What is the greatest angle at which the table can be tilted before the rubber starts to slide?

3 A climber of mass 65 kg is practising traversing a slab of rock. The coefficient of friction between her feet and the rock is 1.2.

(a) What is the greatest angle of slope she can walk on?

(b) What is the force due to friction at that point?

4 A sledge of mass 150 kg is being held on a snowy slope by a rope parallel to the slope. If the slope makes an angle of 35° to the horizontal and the coefficient of static friction is 0.02, what is the least force required

(a) to hold it stationary

(b) to start it moving up the slope?

5 A climber of mass 100 kg is being held stationary on a rough slope of angle 80° to the horizontal by his partner at the top of the slope.

If the coefficient of static friction between the climber and the slope is 0.9, what are the limits on the tension in the rope?

F Models of sliding friction (answers p. 158)

When you solve problems you generally need to make assumptions about the forces which act. In particular, you need to have reasonable 'models' for friction, tension and air resistance in various situations. A 'reasonable model' for a force involves making assumptions about the force which experience tells you have worked well in similar situations. Scientists and engineers have collected a number of 'standard models' of this kind which are now in common use, though it is *impossible to guarantee* that they will work in any new situation and they are usually only approximately true. In Section E you looked at a model for static friction. Here you will consider friction when objects are sliding.

Problem

What model of friction would be
appropriate for a curling stone
travelling along the ice?

The data below were collected for a curling stone from the moment it
left the curler's hand until it came to rest.

Displacement x (metres)	0	5	10	15	20	25	30	35	40
Time t (seconds)	0	2.5	5.5	8.5	11.9	16.2	21.7	31.1	–

Set up a model

Assume that the stone is a particle of
mass m kg and that air resistance can
be ignored. Let the friction force be F
and the velocity be $v \, \mathrm{m\,s^{-1}}$.

The key assumption concerns the
friction F. First, try the model $F = 0$.

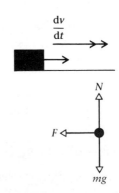

Model 1: Sliding friction is zero

Analyse the problem

Apply Newton's second law taking the x-axis to be horizontal and the
y-axis vertical:

$$\begin{bmatrix} -F \\ N - mg \end{bmatrix} = m \begin{bmatrix} \dfrac{\mathrm{d}v}{\mathrm{d}t} \\ 0 \end{bmatrix}$$

$F = 0$ and so $\dfrac{\mathrm{d}v}{\mathrm{d}t} = 0$

Therefore v is a constant, u, say.
Then $x = ut$.

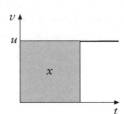

Interpret/validate

The stone continues to slide at speed u for ever.

In fact this result is a reasonable model for the first 20 metres of the motion.

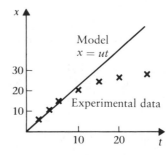

1 Find a value for u which best fits the first 20 metres of the motion.

You can see that the model does not fit the data well for values of t greater than 10 seconds.

It is clear that the graph of (t, x) should be a curve.

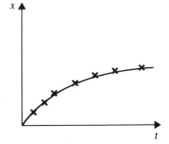

2 What conclusion should you reach about the model $F = 0$
   (a) for the first few seconds of the motion
   (b) for the motion when $t > 10$ seconds?

You can now refine the model for the second part of the motion.

Set up a model

The only assumption you need to change is $F = 0$.
Now let F be constant throughout the motion.

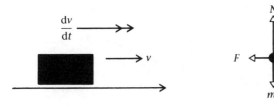

Model 2: Sliding friction is constant during the motion

Analyse the problem

Applying Newton's second law,

$$\begin{bmatrix} -F \\ N-mg \end{bmatrix} = m \begin{bmatrix} \dfrac{dv}{dt} \\ 0 \end{bmatrix}$$

Therefore, $-F = m\dfrac{dv}{dt}$ and $N - mg = 0$

so $\dfrac{dv}{dt} = \dfrac{-F}{m}$

Integrating gives $v = u - \dfrac{Ft}{m}$ and $x = ut - \dfrac{Ft^2}{2m}$

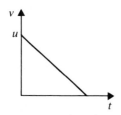

Interpret/validate

The stone comes to rest after $t = \dfrac{um}{F}$ seconds.

The faster it is projected, the longer it takes to stop. It is clear that after this point the model becomes invalid.

You must now match the equation

$$x = ut - \dfrac{F}{2m}t^2$$

against the data collected previously.

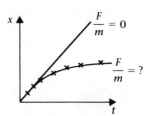

3   (a)   What value of $\dfrac{F}{m}$ will give a reasonable fit for this set of data?

(b)   What can you conclude about the model $F =$ constant for a stone sliding until it comes to rest?

Sliding friction

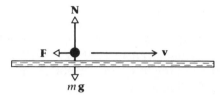

The friction force always acts in the direction opposed to the velocity of the body relative to the surface of contact.

(a) $F = 0$ if the object is moving on a smooth surface (e.g. a puck on ice for a short period of time).

(b) $F = \mu_D N$ where μ_D is the coefficient of sliding friction ('D' stands for dynamic) and N is the normal contact force

μ_D is normally less than μ_S for any two bodies in contact.

Example 6

A box of mass 20 kg is being pushed across a rough floor at constant velocity by a horizontal force of 20 newtons. Using the model for sliding friction $F = \mu N$, what is the coefficient of sliding friction μ?

What force must be used if the mass of the box is doubled?

Solution

Let the friction be F and the normal contact force be N. The box does not accelerate vertically or horizontally, so by Newton's second law,

$$N = 200 \text{ N} \quad \text{and} \quad F = 20 \text{ N}$$

Then $F = \mu N \implies \mu = 0.1$.

If the mass of the box is doubled, N is doubled and $F = 0.1 \times 400 = 40$. The push must then be 40 newtons horizontally.

Exercise F (answers p. 158)

1   A block of mass 6 kg will move at constant velocity when pushed along a table by a horizontal force of 24 N. Find the coefficient of friction between the block and the table.

2   A puck of mass 0.1 kg is sliding in a straight line on an ice rink. The coefficient of sliding friction between the puck and the ice is 0.02. Find the resistive force due to friction and then find the speed of the puck after 20 seconds if its initial speed is 10 m s^{-1}.

3   A particle of mass 1 kg is projected at 5 m s^{-1} along a rough horizontal surface. The coefficient of sliding friction is 0.3. Assuming that $F = \mu N$, how far does the particle move before coming to rest?

4   A box of mass 5 kg is pulled across the floor by the tension in a string attached to it. The string makes an angle of 40° with the horizontal. What is the acceleration of the box if the tension in the string is 60 N and the coefficient of friction is 0.6?

5E A rough plane is inclined at an angle ϕ to the horizontal.

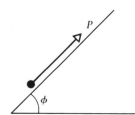

A particle slides down the slope at constant speed when an additional force P is applied as shown.

Show that $P = mg(\sin \phi - \mu \cos \phi)$ where m is the mass of the particle and μ is the coefficient of friction.

If the additional force is trebled to $3P$, and the particle now moves up the plane with constant speed, show that $\tan \phi = 2\mu$.

After working through this chapter you should

1   be able to find the resultant of several forces on a particle

2   be able to use this resultant to find the acceleration of the particle

3   know that if a particle is in equilibrium then the resultant force acting on it is zero; a particle that is in equilibrium will either remain at rest or travel with constant velocity

4   be able to resolve a force, **F**, into two components, $F \sin \phi$ and $F \cos \phi$

5   be able to model situations involving friction, tension and resistance.

10 Connected bodies

A Static two-body problems (answers p. 159)

Newton's third law tells us that for every force there exists an equal and opposite force. Let us see how this works.

1D (a) A book of mass 2 kg is placed on a 3 kg block. The two bodies are at rest on a horizontal table, as in the diagram, while the book is pushed to the right by a horizontal 5 N force. Show the forces on each body separately. Take $g = 10$ m s^{-2}.

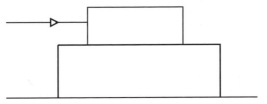

(b) The push is increased until there is movement. If the coefficient of friction between the book and the block is 0.4, and that between the block and the table is 0.2, find where slipping takes place.

Example 1

Three lights are hung symmetrically from points B, C, D on a wire crossing a village hall. BC and CD are at 50° to the vertical, while AB is at 20° to the vertical. The central light has mass 3 kg. Find the tensions in AB and BC and the mass of the light suspended from B.

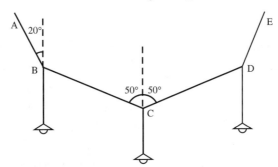

Solution

We will assume that the weight of the wires can be neglected compared with the weights of the lights. The diagrams below show the forces on B and C and also the forces on the wire BC.

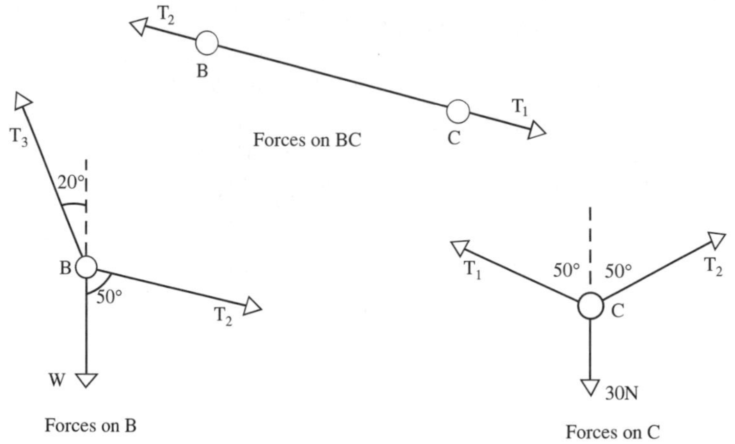

Forces on BC

Forces on B

Forces on C

We may imagine small rings at B and C. The force on the wire BC at B is equal and opposite to the force that the wire exerts on the ring at B. Similarly at C.

If BC had been a heavy chain, it would have hung in a curve and the forces on it at B and C would have been different. As it is, the middle diagram shows that $T_2 = T_1$.

Vertical components at C give $2T_1 \cos 50° = 30$, $T_1 = 23.3$ N.

Horizontal components at B give $T_3 \sin 20° = T_2 \sin 50°$, so $T_3 = 52.3$ N since $T_2 = T_1$.

Vertical components at B give $T_3 \cos 20° = W + T_2 \cos 50°$, and hence $W = 34.1$ N.

The required mass is 3.4 kg.

Internal and external forces

In the problems above, we can consider each body separately or, alternatively, two or more bodies together. Thus in Example 1, considering vertical components overall we get

$$2T_3 \cos 20° = 30 + 2W.$$

In this case, the tensions in BC and CD are **internal forces** and cancel out, but the weights and the tensions in AB and DE are **external forces**. Similarly, in question 1D we can see that the normal reaction provided by the table is 50 N by considering the book and block together.

2D Look back at experiments (c) and (d) on p. 2. List some of the external and internal forces in each situation and explain what happens in each case.

(c) A friend holds a bicycle upright.
What happens if you push backwards on the lower pedal?

(d) What happens when you stand on a set of bathroom scales and press down with a broom (i) on the scales, (ii) on the floor?

Exercise A (answers p. 160)

Take $g = 10 \text{ m s}^{-2}$.

1 Two bodies are suspended from the ceiling as shown. Find the tensions in the two strings.

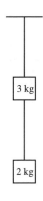

2

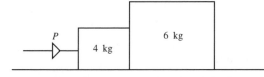

Two boxes lie side by side on the floor. The coefficient of friction is 0.3 between the smaller box and the floor, and 0.7 between the larger box and the floor. Find the minimum horizontal force P needed to make the boxes slide and the normal contact force then between the boxes. Draw diagrams to show the forces on the two boxes separately.

3 What would the normal contact force be in question 2 if P were applied to the 6 kg box instead?

4 A 2 kg book is placed on a 3 kg block on a horizontal table, as in Section A. When the table is tipped through 10°, there is no slipping. Find the friction force between the book and the block, and the friction force between the block and the table.

Find the normal contact forces. What can you say about the coefficients of friction?

5 You are a passenger in a car. Discuss the internal forces between you and the car when

(a) the car is accelerated fast

(b) the car is braked sharply.

B Connected bodies in motion (answers p. 160)

The interaction principle must be used whenever the motion of two or more connected bodies is analysed.

1 A man of mass 70 kg is in a lift of mass 500 kg which is accelerating upwards at 2 m s^{-2}.

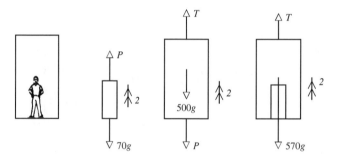

(a) The second diagram shows the forces on the man. Use it to find the force exerted by the floor on the man.

(b) The third diagram shows the forces on the lift alone, while the fourth shows the external forces on the man and lift combined. Show that both these diagrams give $T = 6840$ N (taking $g = 10$ m s^{-2}).

(c) What can you say about the values of P

    (i) when the lift is ascending at steady speed

    (ii) when it slows down

    (iii) during the descent?

Example 2

A 5 kg mass on a fixed rough table ($\mu = 0.4$) is connected to a mass of 3 kg hanging freely by a string passing over a small, well-oiled pulley at the edge of the table. What happens when the system is released?

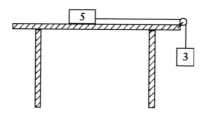

Solution

At all times, the two bodies have equal speeds and so their accelerations are equal in magnitude. The tension of the string is the same all along its length. These facts enable us to produce diagrams for the bodies separately.

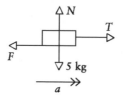   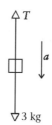

Now from the first diagram,

$$T - F = 5a \qquad \text{and} \qquad N = 5g.$$

From the second diagram,

$$3g - T = 3a.$$

Since also $F = 0.4N = 2g$, it follows that

$$a = \tfrac{1}{8}g = 1.25 \text{ m s}^{-2}, \qquad \text{taking } g = 10 \text{ m s}^{-2},$$

and $T = 26.25$ N.

Notice that during the motion, the tension has a value smaller than the weight of the hanging mass but larger than the frictional force.

If the mass on the table had been 10 kg instead of 5 kg, no motion would have taken place. Both T and F would then have the value $3g = 30$ N.

Exercise B (answers p. 160)

Take $g = 10$ m s^{-2}.

1 Outside any gravitational field, a force of 300 N is pushing a mass of 56 kg against another of 144 kg. What is the thrust between the two masses?

2   A lorry of mass 2000 kg is towing a car of mass 1300 kg connected to it by a steel bar. In slowing down, the force along the tow bar is 1000 N. What is the magnitude of the retarding force on the system if it is

(a) entirely due to the car

(b) entirely due to the lorry?

3   A load of mass 40 kg is retarded at 6 m s^{-2} by a newly opened parachute of mass 2 kg. If the air resistance to the load is 30 N, what vertical forces does the parachute exert on it, and what is the air resistance to the parachute?

4   A man of mass 90 kg is in the cabin suspended below a balloon, and the total mass of the balloon and cabin (excluding the man) is 800 kg. A steady downward drift at 8 m s^{-1} is stopped by throwing out 50 kg of ballast. What is the change in the upward force on the man's feet when the ballast is jettisoned? What will be the speed of the balloon 30 seconds later?

5   A lift of mass 1 tonne carrying a load of 200 kg is descending at 4 m s^{-1}, and slowing down. If the tension in the supporting cables is 13 000 N find the contact force between the load and the lift floor. How much further will the lift descend before coming to rest?

6   Masses of 3 kg and 5 kg are at the ends of a light string which passes over a smooth fixed peg. Calculate the accelerations of the bodies and the tension in the string.

7   A block of mass 10 kg rests on a horizontal table, the coefficient of friction between block and table being 0.3. The block is attached to a hanging mass of M kg by a string which passes over a smoothly running pulley at the edge of the table.

(a) Draw diagrams to show the forces on
    (i)   the block
    (ii) the hanging mass.

(b) Find the tension in the string and say what will happen when
    (i) $M = 2$ (ii) $M = 4$.

After working through this chapter you should

1   be able to distinguish between internal and external forces

2   be able to draw separate diagrams showing the forces on the constituents of a two-body system

3   be able to apply $\mathbf{F} = m\mathbf{a}$ to a two-body problem.

Answers

1 Modelling motion

A Introduction (p. 1)

1D You are *not* expected to provide the correct theoretical explanations at this stage. The point of these investigations is to direct your attention to the interesting questions you can ask about the world of mechanics and motion in which we live.

(a) The balls will hit the ground simultaneously.

(b) The full can takes the shorter time to roll down the slope. (However, a half-full can does not take a time halfway between those taken by the full and the empty cans.)

(c) The bicycle will roll backwards, but the pedal will rotate forwards. Try the experiment yourself.

(d) (i) The reading stays the same.
(ii) The reading decreases.

Perpetual motion machines, the swirling of bathwater down a plughole and road banking angles are just a few of the many other interesting ideas you may have considered. Further examples are described in the following books:

Epstein, L. C., *Thinking Physics Is Gedanken Physics*, Insight, San Francisco, 1983.
Walker, J., *The Flying Circus of Physics*, J. Wein, New York, 1975.

2D The aim of the experiment is to find the relationship between time taken and distance rolled. It is important at this stage to learn the art of good experimental practice! Some important points to remember are:

Consistency
It is important that each result is obtained by a set procedure, so that the experiment is repeatable. If a ball rolls 1 metre down the track in 2.2 seconds the first time, the experiment should be repeated to test how consistent this time is (within the degree of accuracy concerned). If the ball bounces from side to side, or if the measuring is done in a sloppy and inconsistent manner (for example, from the front of the ball one time and the middle the next), then you should expect inconsistent results.

The following points may help.

(a) Call out '3, 2, 1, go' as you release the ball and let the ball hit a brick at the end of its measured run.

(b) Use a brick to hold the ball in place at the start. This will help you to get the correct distance between the start and the finish.

Accuracy
What sources of inaccuracy are there? For example, in measuring time, there are delayed reactions. Can these cancel each other out at the beginning and end of the run?

The experiment should be set up to take at least 3 seconds for the ball to roll the full length of the track.

Consider the use of the mean, mode or median in choosing which measurement to use in your analysis.

Galileo had difficulty measuring time accurately and records show that he had to design a special time-piece; he used a large flat vessel of water from which water was allowed to drip, the weight of the water released being measured to give the time.

Repeatability
The data collected *must* be repeatable by other experimenters at other times. It is essential, therefore, to note all pertinent details, for example

- type of track and ball
- angle of slope
- length of track
- method of timing.

Analysis
Having collected the data, a graph can be drawn and a function fitted to it. The points should be joined by some type of curve. A function graph plotter can be used.

The ball starts from rest and travels with increasing speed down the track. The results should give an approximation to $d = kt^2$. The shape of the graph is indicated below. As the slope of the track is increased, k increases. However, if the angle of the track is too great then it becomes impossible to measure t with accuracy. (Any result using a value of t smaller than 0.5 seconds is suspect.)

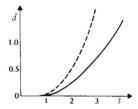

Interpretation and validation
The experiment should not stop here, but should be followed by

- prediction of a given time for a roll of given distance, within the range of distances recorded (interpolation)
- validation of predictions by testing them practically.

B   Applied mathematical modelling
(p. 2)

You may not understand any of the theory behind the experiments at this point. You must, however, learn how to record and interpret your results. The actual mechanics behind the answers will be explained at the appropriate point in the chapter. You will then refer back to the results you obtained here and see how they fit into the theory.

It is important that data for the experiments are collected and kept for later use.

1   Some practical details are:

- The pulley should be fixed securely in a vertical plane with the string moving freely without knots or snagging on the pulley.
- The system should be released from rest each time. This is easy to do if the string is held at the pulley and then released on the word 'Go'.
- Several runs will be needed to assess consistency and accuracy; obviously poor runs should be excluded.

Other practical problems may be encountered and you should learn how to solve them yourself.

The results should give a clear graph of time increasing with distance.

If the distances measured are great, the masses may reach a steady 'terminal' velocity due to the friction in the pulley.

If the distances are too small, then inaccuracies in timing may hide any clear relationship between distance and time. If friction is ignored, a relationship of the form $d = kt^2$ is expected.

Possible extensions include changing the masses, for example to 50 g and 60 g, and repeating the investigation.

You should make use of the modelling diagram in writing up your results.

2   Check for accuracy and consistency as before. Release from the same point each time, choosing a point from which the ball takes at least 3 seconds to roll 1 metre.

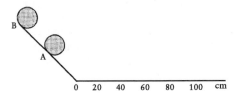

In the initial experiment the results depend on whether the times are measured from the release point A, or from when the ball reaches the start of the track at 0. They are shown by the thinner and thicker lines in the graph. The release point also affects the gradient of the graph.

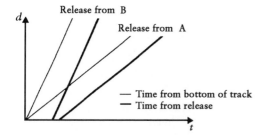

The second set of data collected for the ball rolling along the felt or ribbon can be used later to find the friction force involved. In this case, the (t, d) graph will not be linear as the ball will soon come to rest on the track.

3   The horizontal line at the base of the plane should pass through the base of the ramp as shown below. Release points 1 and 2 are too low to give a curve that fits most of the paper. Once again, to be consistent you must always release the ball from exactly the same height.

Care must be taken to avoid soaking the sugar paper with water or the ball will not roll properly.

The path traced out should be a parabola in all cases.

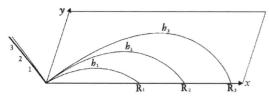

Discrepancies are caused by energy loss through friction or malformation of the ball. A snooker ball is probably best. The graph should have an equation of the form $y = kr(R - x)$, where R is the range.

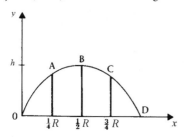

The release height is proportional to both h and R. It is also proportional to the square of the velocity at the bottom of the ramp.

If a ruler is laid across the path, then the times for the ball to travel through equal horizontal distances across the table can be found. This should show that the horizontal component of speed is constant.

2   Kinematics

A   Motion (p. 9)

1D   Distance, speed and time are represented; acceleration, engine revolutions, steering wheel position and many other relevant aspects are not.

B   Average speed (p. 10)

1D   Overall average speed does not mean the average of the different speeds. It means the constant speed at which the person must travel in order to travel the same total distance in the same time.

Exercise B (p. 12)

1   Distance covered in first 30 seconds
= 150 metres

Distance covered in second 30 seconds
= 60 metres

Average speed $= \dfrac{150 + 60}{30 + 30} = 3.5 \text{ m s}^{-1}$

2   Average speed $= \dfrac{150 + 150}{30 + 75} = 2.9 \text{ m s}^{-1}$

3   2.25 m s^{-1}

4   The total time for the journey was $\frac{210}{42} = 5$ hours. The time for the first half of the journey's distance was $\frac{105}{30} = 3.5$ hours and so the average speed for the second half was $\frac{105}{1.5} = 70$ miles per hour (31.3 m s^{-1}).

5E $\dfrac{30u + 30v}{60} = \dfrac{u + v}{2} \text{ m s}^{-1}$

You can use the arithmetic average of the speeds if the jogger runs and walks for equal lengths of time.

6E Running: $30u$ metres in 30 seconds

Walking: $30u$ metres in $\dfrac{30u}{v}$ seconds

Average speed $= \dfrac{30u + 30u}{30 + \dfrac{30u}{v}} = \dfrac{2uv}{u + v}$ m s^{-1}

C (Time, distance) and (time, speed) graphs (p. 12)

1D The gradient, $\dfrac{ds}{dt}$, of a (t, s) graph represents speed. The corresponding $\left(t, \dfrac{ds}{dt}\right)$ graphs would show that the under-18 winner is faster.

The model is unrealistic because an athlete does not travel at a constant speed from the beginning to the end of a race.

2 (a) There are many possible explanations of the shape of the graph.

(b)

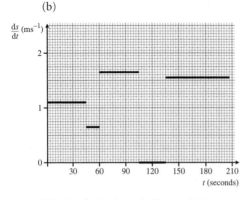

(c) On the (t, s) graph, the total distance of 250 metres is the height of the final point. On the $\left(t, \dfrac{ds}{dt}\right)$ graph it is the sum of the areas under the horizontal line segments.

(d) The fact that the lecturer was stationary is represented by a horizontal line on the (t, s) graph and by the graph running along the t-axis on the $\left(t, \dfrac{ds}{dt}\right)$ graph.

(e) The lecturer travelled most quickly in the interval from 60 to 105 seconds. The (t, s) graph has its steepest gradient, and the $\left(t, \dfrac{ds}{dt}\right)$ graph is highest for this interval.

Exercise C (p. 15)

1 Distance covered $= 2250$ m (or 2.25 km)

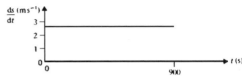

A simple model would represent her stopping by a discontinuity (or break) in the (time, speed) graph at $t = 900$ as shown above. More realistically the graph might be shaped as shown.

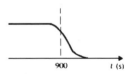

2 Running distance $= 4.8 \times 60 = 288$ metres

Jogging distance $= 3.0 \times 90 = 270$ metres

Total distance covered is

$20 \times (288 + 270) = 11\,160$ metres

3

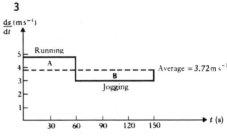

Note that area A and area B are equal.

4 (a)

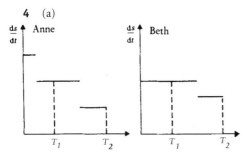

Anne set off quickly but soon slowed down and then finished the race at an even slower pace. Beth maintained a steady pace for most of the race (the same as Anne's middle pace) and then slowed down to a somewhat higher finishing pace than Anne. They finished the race together.

(b) At T_1 they have the same speed. The (t, s) graphs have equal gradients; the $\left(t, \dfrac{ds}{dt}\right)$ graphs have the same heights.

(c) At T_2, they have covered the same distance. The (t, s) graphs have equal heights; the areas under the $\left(t, \dfrac{ds}{dt}\right)$ graphs are equal.

5 Distance to motorway = 61 560 m

Distance on motorway = 116 640 m

Distance after motorway = 28 890 m

Total distance = 207.09 km (say 207 km)

6

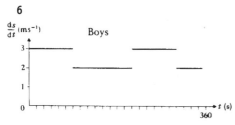

In 1 hour the boys completed 16 repetitions of (2×270) m, i.e. 8640 m.

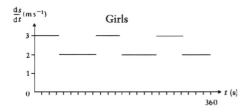

In 58 minutes 20 seconds the girls completed 28 repetitions of (2×150) m, i.e. 8400 m. In the remaining 100 seconds the girls completed the 150 m running phase and walked for 50 seconds at 2 m s^{-1}, covering a further 250 m. The girls therefore won by 10 metres.

D Speed (p. 16)

1 (a) The ball's speed $\dfrac{ds}{dt}$ at that instant is 0.64 m s^{-1}. If its speed remained constant at 0.64 m s^{-1}, then its (t, s) graph would follow the dashed tangent from 2 seconds onwards.

(b)

Time in seconds	0.5	1	1.5	2	2.5	3
Gradient	0.16	0.32	0.48	0.64	0.80	0.96

(c) The $\left(t, \dfrac{ds}{dt}\right)$ graph is a straight line.

The speed of the ball increases by approximately 0.32 m s^{-1} each second.

If you use your own data, a curve should be drawn and the gradients found.

The $\left(t, \dfrac{ds}{dt}\right)$ points found using your gradients may not lie exactly on a line but you should have a set of points giving a good approximation to a straight line through the origin.

Exercise D (p. 18)

1 (a) The area under the curve between $t = 10$ and $t = 15$ is just less than 75 metres. The speed is increasing but not at a steady rate.

(b) Between $t = 20$ and $t = 25$, the object slows down at a constant rate until it is stationary. The distance covered each second decreases. A total distance of 50 metres is covered in this period.

2   Each 1 cm grid square represents 20 metres and each small square represents $\frac{20}{25} = 0.8$ metres.

Estimates to 2 s.f. are:

(a)   130 metres
(b)   380 metres

3   B starts 2 seconds later than A from the same point and walks in the same direction but at a greater speed. B covers $3 \times 3 = 9$ metres.
A and B therefore meet 9 metres from the start. A's speed is $\frac{9}{5} = 1.8$ m s^{-1}.

4

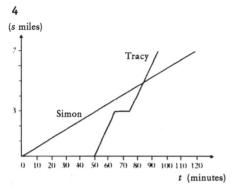

(*s* miles)

Tracy

Simon

t (minutes)

(a)   Approximately 2 miles from Ceville.

(b) $7 \div 46 = 0.152$ miles per minute
$0.152 \times 60 \approx 9.1$ m.p.h.

(c) $7 \div 2 = 3.5$ m.p.h.

[It is assumed that when travelling they both maintain a constant speed.]

5   (a)   From $t = 2$ to $t = 5$, speed increases uniformly from 2 to 8 m s^{-1}. Using areas,

when $t = 3$, $\dfrac{ds}{dt} = 4$ and
$s = 4 + \frac{1}{2}(2 + 4) = 7$;

when $t = 4$, $\dfrac{ds}{dt} = 6$ and
$s = 7 + \frac{1}{2}(4 + 6) = 12$;

when $t = 5$, $\dfrac{ds}{dt} = 8$ and
$s = 12 + \frac{1}{2}(6 + 8) = 19$

(b)   The distance covered is 19 metres.

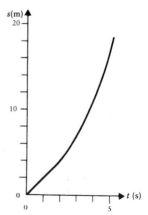

s(m)

t (s)

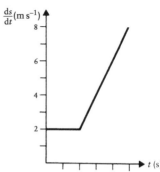

$\dfrac{ds}{dt}$(m s^{-1})

t (s)

6   (a)   A moves at constant speed.

(b)   B moves with a constant rate of increase of speed, up to twice the speed of A.

(c)   After 2 seconds.

(d)   After 4 seconds.

E   Investigations involving speed
(p. 20)

1D   A 'two-second gap' means that if there is a gap of 50 metres, say, between the front of your car and the rear of the car in front it should take you at least two seconds to cover that distance. This means that you should not be travelling at more than 25 m s^{-1}.

2   **Set up a model**
Assume

- the car has length 5 m and is moving at a constant speed of V m s^{-1}

- the lorry has length 15 m and is moving with constant speed U m s^{-1}

- they obey the two-second rule
- the car takes t seconds to overtake.

Analyse the problem

The car must travel $(5 + 2V + 15 + 2U)$ m if the lorry is stationary. But the lorry will have travelled Ut metres in that time, so the total overtaking distance in metres is $20 + 2(U + V) + Ut$.

But the car has travelled Vt metres, so

$$Vt = 20 + 2(U + V) + Ut$$
$$\Rightarrow \quad t(V - U) = 20 + 2(U + V)$$
$$t = \frac{20 + 2(U + V)}{V - U}$$

The distance travelled, s, is

$$s = Vt = \frac{2V(10 + U + V)}{(V - U)}$$

Interpret/validate

As $V - U$ increases, s decreases. The greater the difference in speed, the smaller the distance needed.

As V increases, the car must pull out earlier if it is not to break the two-second rule. However, the overall passing distance decreases unless V is much bigger than U.

The greater the combined speeds of the two, the greater the distance. If $U > V$ then s is negative i.e. passing is impossible. If $U = 0$ then the distance is $20 + 2V$.

3 Vectors

A Introduction (p. 24)

1D Time, distance, speed and mass are scalar quantities that we shall be much concerned with. There are many others.

Similarly, velocity, acceleration, force and momentum are all vector quantities we shall use later.

Exercise A (p. 27)

(Answers are given to 1 decimal place where necessary.)

1 (a)

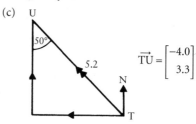

$$\overrightarrow{PQ} = \begin{bmatrix} 7 \sin 60° \\ 7 \cos 60° \end{bmatrix} \approx \begin{bmatrix} 6.1 \\ 3.5 \end{bmatrix}$$

(b)

$$\overrightarrow{RS} = \begin{bmatrix} -4.1 \\ -11.3 \end{bmatrix}$$

(c)

$$\overrightarrow{TU} = \begin{bmatrix} -4.0 \\ 3.3 \end{bmatrix}$$

2 (a) $AB = \sqrt{5^2 + 12^2} = 13$

$\tan \alpha = \frac{5}{12} \Rightarrow \alpha \approx 22.6°$

The bearing is $022.6°$.

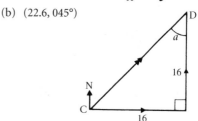

(b) $(22.6, 045°)$

(c) $(10.1, 212.9°)$

(d) $(5, 143.1°)$

3 846 m east, 172 m south; $281°$; assuming there is no current.

4 57 cm at $-12°$ to the x-axis

B   Vectors and maps (p. 27)

1D (a) 033498 016409 (taken at the middle)
(b) Dairy,   The Bite
(c) (2.4, 47.3),   (3.2, 50.5)

Exercise B (p. 30)

1 (a) Distance from C to B
$= \sqrt{12.7^2 + 20.1^2} \approx 23.8$ km

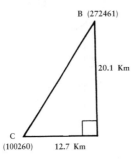

B (272461)

20.1 Km

C
(100260)   12.7 Km

(b) $\tan \alpha = \dfrac{6.3}{29.7} \implies \alpha \approx 12.0°$

The bearing of D from A is about 102°.

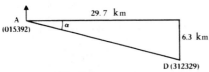

29.7 km

A
(015392)   α

6.3 km

D (312329)

(c) $\overrightarrow{BD} = \begin{bmatrix} 8.5 \\ -13.2 \end{bmatrix}$

$\overrightarrow{BD}$ is 15.7 km on a bearing of 147.2°.

(d) The bearing of $\overrightarrow{DB}$ is
147.2° + 180° = 327.2°.

(e) $\overrightarrow{AB} = \begin{bmatrix} 21.2 \\ 6.9 \end{bmatrix}$ $\overrightarrow{CD} = \begin{bmatrix} 21.2 \\ 6.9 \end{bmatrix}$

Hence $\overrightarrow{AB} = \overrightarrow{CD} \implies AB = CD$, and
AB is in the same direction as CD.

2 318358

3 Ayton is 14.0 km from Botton, on a
bearing of 312° (both to 3 s.f.).

C   Adding vectors (p. 30)

1D For practical purposes, such as the flight of
an aeroplane or the movement of a ship,
the sensible way of representing a
displacement is by distance and bearing.

However, if displacements are to be
combined, it is generally easier if column
vectors are used.

Hence the usefulness of the form of vector
depends on the purpose for which it is
required.

2 (a) $\overrightarrow{XZ} = \begin{bmatrix} 18.5 - \ 2.6 \\ 49.6 - 10.2 \end{bmatrix} = \begin{bmatrix} 15.9 \\ 39.4 \end{bmatrix}$

$\overrightarrow{XY} = \begin{bmatrix} 10.8 \\ 5.2 \end{bmatrix}$ $\overrightarrow{YZ} = \begin{bmatrix} 5.1 \\ 34.2 \end{bmatrix}$

(b) The sum of the eastwards
components of $\overrightarrow{XY}$ and $\overrightarrow{YZ}$ is
10.8 + 5.1 = 15.9, which equals the
eastwards component of $\overrightarrow{XZ}$.

Also the sum of the northwards
components of $\overrightarrow{XY}$ and $\overrightarrow{YZ}$ is
5.2 + 34.2 = 39.4 which equals the
northwards component of $\overrightarrow{XZ}$.
Therefore you can write
$\overrightarrow{XZ} = \overrightarrow{XY} + \overrightarrow{YZ}$.

(c) (i) $XZ \approx 42.5$ $\alpha \approx 22.0°$

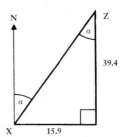

N   Z

α

39.4

α

X   15.9

In going from X to Z the
helicopter flies a distance of
42.5 km in the direction 022.0°.

(ii) In going from X to Y it flies a
distance of 12.0 km in the
direction 064.3°.

(iii) In going from Y to Z it flies a
distance of 34.6 km in direction
008.5°.

3 $\overrightarrow{AB} = \begin{bmatrix} 4 \\ -2 \end{bmatrix}$, $\overrightarrow{BC} = \begin{bmatrix} 2 \\ 6 \end{bmatrix}$, $\overrightarrow{AC} = \begin{bmatrix} 6 \\ 4 \end{bmatrix}$

Notice that $\overrightarrow{AB} + \overrightarrow{BC} = \begin{bmatrix} 4 \\ -2 \end{bmatrix} + \begin{bmatrix} 2 \\ 6 \end{bmatrix}$

$= \begin{bmatrix} 6 \\ 4 \end{bmatrix} = \overrightarrow{AC}$

4 $\overrightarrow{AD} = \overrightarrow{AB} + \overrightarrow{BC} + \overrightarrow{CD}$

$$= \begin{bmatrix} 2 \\ 2 \end{bmatrix} + \begin{bmatrix} 2 \\ 0 \end{bmatrix} + \begin{bmatrix} 3 \\ -4 \end{bmatrix} = \begin{bmatrix} 7 \\ -2 \end{bmatrix}$$

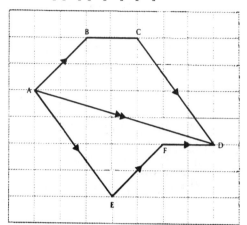

5 $\overrightarrow{AD} = \overrightarrow{AE} + \overrightarrow{EF} + \overrightarrow{FD}$

$$= \begin{bmatrix} 3 \\ -4 \end{bmatrix} + \begin{bmatrix} 2 \\ 2 \end{bmatrix} + \begin{bmatrix} 2 \\ 0 \end{bmatrix} = \begin{bmatrix} 7 \\ -2 \end{bmatrix}$$

Notice that the resultant is the same, irrespective of the order in which the vectors are added.

Exercise C (p. 33)

1 $\begin{bmatrix} 3 \\ -1 \end{bmatrix} + \begin{bmatrix} -2 \\ 4 \end{bmatrix} = \begin{bmatrix} 1 \\ 3 \end{bmatrix}$

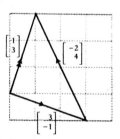

2 (a) $\mathbf{u} + \mathbf{v}$ (b) $\mathbf{u} + 2\mathbf{v}$ (c) $\mathbf{v} - \mathbf{u}$

3 $\begin{bmatrix} -2 \\ -3 \end{bmatrix} + \begin{bmatrix} 5 \\ -7 \end{bmatrix} + \begin{bmatrix} 16 \\ 4 \end{bmatrix} = \begin{bmatrix} 19 \\ -6 \end{bmatrix}$

Missing vector $= \begin{bmatrix} -9 \\ 4 \end{bmatrix}$

4 (a) $\overrightarrow{BC} = \begin{bmatrix} 19.5 - 10.5 \\ 40 \ - 15.5 \end{bmatrix} = \begin{bmatrix} 9 \\ 24.5 \end{bmatrix}$

$\overrightarrow{AD} = \overrightarrow{BC} = \begin{bmatrix} 9 \\ 24.5 \end{bmatrix}$

(b) D is (115350)

(c) $\overrightarrow{AB} = \overrightarrow{DC} = \begin{bmatrix} 8.0 \\ 5.0 \end{bmatrix}$

$\Rightarrow$ ABCD is a parallelogram.

D Using vectors (p. 33)

Exercise D (p. 35)

1 $\overrightarrow{PQ} = \begin{bmatrix} -100 \cos 45° \\ 100 \sin 45° \end{bmatrix} \approx \begin{bmatrix} -70.7 \\ 70.7 \end{bmatrix}$

$\overrightarrow{AQ} = \begin{bmatrix} 12.3 \\ 70.7 \end{bmatrix}$

$|\overrightarrow{AQ}| \approx 71.8$

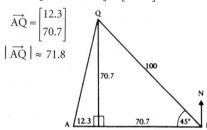

Airport Q is closer to the aircraft by 11.2 km.

2 $\overrightarrow{PS} = \begin{bmatrix} 15.97 \\ -12.04 \end{bmatrix}$ $\overrightarrow{HS} \approx \begin{bmatrix} 10.97 \\ -12.04 \end{bmatrix}$

$|\overrightarrow{HS}| \approx 16.3$ $\theta \approx 47.7°$

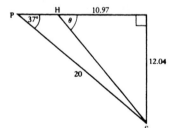

The helicopter has to fly in the direction 137.7° for a distance of 16.3 km.

3 The displacement westwards of the boat is 9 sin 38° km each hour and the time taken for its displacement westwards to be

4.7 km is $\dfrac{4.7}{9 \sin 38°} \approx 0.85$ hour =

= 51 minutes

Hence it will be due north of Black Cap Light at 3:06 a.m.

4 The helicopter has to fly 33.6 km in the direction 266.6°.

5 The displacement of HMS *Battledore* from port at 15:00 is

$$\frac{2}{5}\begin{bmatrix} 15\sin 61° \\ -15\cos 61° \end{bmatrix} + \frac{7}{20}\begin{bmatrix} -15\sin 17° \\ 15\cos 17° \end{bmatrix}$$

$$= \begin{bmatrix} 6\sin 61° - 5.25\sin 17° \\ -6\cos 61° + 5.25\cos 17° \end{bmatrix}$$

The displacement of HMS *Shuttlecock* from port at 15:00 is $\begin{bmatrix} -6\sin 25° \\ -6\cos 25° \end{bmatrix}$

The displacement of HMS *Shuttlecock* from HMS *Battledore* is $\begin{bmatrix} -6.25 \\ -7.55 \end{bmatrix}$

$d \approx 9.80$

So at 15:00 the ships are about 9.80 nautical miles apart.

Time taken to meet $\approx \dfrac{9.80}{20} = 0.49$ hour

$$= 29\tfrac{1}{2}\text{ min}$$

$\tan\phi = \dfrac{6.25}{7.55}$

$\Rightarrow \phi \approx 39.6°$
HMS *Battledore* proceeds on bearing 219.6°.

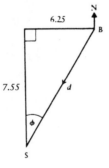

E   Position and displacement (p. 36)

Exercise E (p. 37)

1 (a) The new position vector is

$$\begin{bmatrix} 5.7 \\ 2.6 \end{bmatrix} + \begin{bmatrix} 0.9 \\ 0.2 \end{bmatrix} + \begin{bmatrix} 1.4 \\ -0.7 \end{bmatrix} + \begin{bmatrix} 1.2 \\ 0.5 \end{bmatrix}$$

$$= \begin{bmatrix} 9.2 \\ 2.6 \end{bmatrix}$$

(b) The total displacement is $\begin{bmatrix} 3.5 \\ 0 \end{bmatrix}$.

(c) The boat has travelled

$$\sqrt{0.9^2 + 0.2^2} + \sqrt{1.4^2 + 0.7^2}$$
$$+ \sqrt{1.2^2 + 0.5^2}$$

$$= 0.922 + 1.565 + 1.3$$

$$= 3.79\text{ km} \quad \text{(to 3 s.f.)}$$

2 The displacement is $\begin{bmatrix} 5.36 \\ 16.01 \end{bmatrix}$,

i.e. 16.9 km in the direction 018.5°.

3

	(a)	(b)	(c)	(d)
Original position vector	$\begin{bmatrix} 200 \\ 90 \end{bmatrix}$	$\begin{bmatrix} 7 \\ -7 \end{bmatrix}$	$\begin{bmatrix} -32 \\ 16 \end{bmatrix}$	$\begin{bmatrix} -88 \\ -262 \end{bmatrix}$
New position vector	$\begin{bmatrix} 326 \\ 81 \end{bmatrix}$	$\begin{bmatrix} 73 \\ -81 \end{bmatrix}$	$\begin{bmatrix} -15 \\ -4 \end{bmatrix}$	$\begin{bmatrix} -10 \\ -8 \end{bmatrix}$
Displacement	$\begin{bmatrix} 126 \\ -9 \end{bmatrix}$	$\begin{bmatrix} 66 \\ -74 \end{bmatrix}$	$\begin{bmatrix} 17 \\ -20 \end{bmatrix}$	$\begin{bmatrix} 78 \\ 254 \end{bmatrix}$

4   Velocity

A   Speed or velocity? (p. 39)

1 (a) After slowing down to B, equal distances are covered in equal 10-second time intervals and so the speed seems to be constant throughout the rest of the journey.

(b) For the velocity to be constant the direction of motion has to be in the same straight line *and* the speed must be constant throughout the journey. The part of the journey for which this holds is from E to F.

2 Average speed is obtained by dividing the distance travelled by the time taken to cover that distance. As the road winds from Southlea to Northaven, the distance *along the road* between them is more than 30 km and hence travelling at 60 km h^{-1}, the car will take more than half an hour for the journey.

Average velocity is obtained by dividing the displacement between the start and finish of a journey by the time taken for the journey. The displacement between Southlea and Northaven is 30 km due north. Hence if the average velocity of the second car is 60 km h^{-1} due north, the time taken for the journey is half an hour.

Equivalent constant speed and equivalent constant velocity can only have the same magnitude if the motion is wholly in a straight line in a given direction.

Exercise A (p. 40)

1 Time for outward journey $= \frac{20}{40} = 0.5$ hour

Time for return journey $= \frac{20}{80} = 0.25$ hour

Time for total journey $= 0.75$ hour

Total distance covered $= 40$ km

Average speed $= \frac{40}{0.75}$ km h$^{-1} \approx 53.3$ km h^{-1}

2 Time taken over first stage $= 1$ hour

Time taken to travel d km of second

stage $= \dfrac{d}{60}$ hours

Total length of journey $= (30 + d)$ km

Total time of journey $= \left(1 + \dfrac{d}{60}\right)$ hours

Hence

$$45\left(1 + \frac{d}{60}\right) = 30 + d$$

$$\Rightarrow d = 60$$

Length of second stage $= 60$ km

3 Time taken to go from A to B
$= 30 + 20 + 10 = 60$ seconds

Total distance $= 120$ m

Average speed $= \frac{120}{60}$ m s$^{-1} = 2$ m s^{-1}

Total displacement $= 60$ m due north

Average velocity $= 1$ m s^{-1} due north

4 An object travelling at constant speed, for example a car moving around a curve, will change its direction of motion continuously and hence cannot have constant velocity. However a train travelling along a straight portion of track with constant speed will have constant velocity since its direction of motion is unaltered.

An aircraft flying with constant velocity must be moving with constant speed in a fixed direction.

To sum up, an object travelling with constant speed is not travelling with constant velocity unless the motion takes place in a straight line. On the other hand, a constant velocity means motion in a straight line in a given direction with constant speed; hence constant velocity implies constant speed.

5 If the average velocity is 50 km h^{-1} due east, the end of the journey, B, must be due east of the start A. Unless the car travels due east throughout the journey (when the average speed would be 50 km h^{-1}) the distance travelled must be greater than the length of the straight line AB. Hence the average speed must be at least 50 km h^{-1}.

6 (a) The distance covered by the particle around the semicircular path is $7\pi \approx 22$ m. If the speed increases uniformly with time the average speed is

$$\frac{8 + 14}{2} \text{ m s}^{-1} = 11 \text{ m s}^{-1}$$

Hence the time taken to complete the path is $\frac{22}{11} = 2$ seconds.

(b) The speed is increasing each second by 3 m s^{-1}. Hence it takes 1 second to reach 11 m s^{-1}.

If the distance covered in that one second is d m the average speed is d m s^{-1}.

So $d = \dfrac{8 + 11}{2} = 9\frac{1}{2}$

The particle's speed is 11 m s^{-1} when the particle has travelled $9\frac{1}{2}$ m along the path.

(c) The displacement in travelling from A to B is 14 m in the direction of $\overrightarrow{AB}$ and this takes 2 seconds. Hence the average velocity is 7 m s^{-1} in the direction of $\overrightarrow{AB}$.

7E   Suppose the length of the track is d km.

(a)   The second lap must take

$$\left(\frac{2d}{60} - \frac{d}{40}\right) \text{hours} = \frac{d}{120} \text{hours.}$$

The speed required is 120 km h^{-1}.

(b)   The second lap must now take

$$\left(\frac{2d}{80} - \frac{d}{40}\right) \text{hours} = 0 \text{ hours. This is}$$

impossible.

B   Straight line motion (p. 41)

1

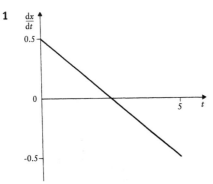

(a)   The graphs show that the furthest distance the ball travels from the bottom of the ramp is 62 cm. The ball is momentarily at rest when $t = 2.5$ seconds. The maximum speed of 0.5 m s^{-1} occurs when $t = 0$ and $t = 5$. The velocity changes from 0.5 m s^{-1} to -0.5 m s^{-1}.

(b)   The area under the $\left(t, \dfrac{dx}{dt}\right)$ graph represents the displacement.

(c)   If the area is underneath the t-axis, then the ball is rolling down the ramp.

(d)   (i) 0.3 m s^{-1} (ii) -0.3 m s^{-1}

(e)   (i) 0.2 m s^{-1} (ii) 0 m s^{-1}

Exercise B (p. 45)

1   (a)   From the (t, x) graph, after 9 seconds the displacement $= 0$.

From the $\left(t, \dfrac{dx}{dt}\right)$ graph for the first T seconds, displacement $= 4T$ metres and for the next $(9 - T)$ seconds, displacement $= -2(9 - T)$ metres.

The total displacement is

$$4T - 2(9 - T) = 6T - 18 = 0 \Longrightarrow T = 3.$$

(b)   When $t = 3$, $x = 12$ so the distance travelled after 9 seconds is $2 \times 12 = 24$ metres.

(c)   The displacement after 9 seconds is 0 metres.

2   (a)   For the motion,

$$x = 6t - 5t^2 \Longrightarrow \frac{dx}{dt} = 6 - 10t$$

When $t = 0.25$, $\dfrac{dx}{dt} = 3.5$

When $t = 2$, $\dfrac{dx}{dt} = -14$

The velocity of the ball after 0.25 seconds is 3.5 m s^{-1} vertically upwards, and after 2 seconds is 14 m s^{-1} vertically downwards.

(b)   The displacement after the first 3 seconds is -27 metres.

$$\text{Average velocity} = \frac{-27}{3} = -9 \text{ m s}^{-1}$$

3   (a)

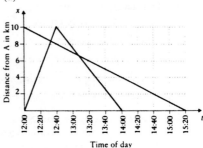

Time of day

(b) $t_1 = 12{:}33$, distance from A ≈ 8.3 km

$t_2 = 13{:}07$, distance from A ≈ 6.7 km

(c) From t_1 to 12:40, the distance apart increases. From 12:40 to t_2, the distance apart decreases. The time when they are the greatest distance apart is 12:40.

4 (a) By calculating gradients it can be established that $\dfrac{dy}{dt} = -10t$ from $t = 0$ to $t = 1.4$.

Between $t = 1.4$ and $t = 3.6$, the graph is symmetrical about $t = 2.5$. You can calculate that $\dfrac{dy}{dt} = 11$ just after $t = 1.4$, and that the graph of $\left(t, \dfrac{dy}{dt}\right)$ is a straight line of gradient -10.

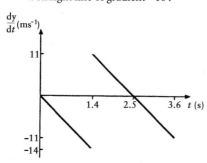

(b) At $t = 1.4$ seconds, the ball hits the ground with a speed of 14 m s^{-1} (velocity -14 m s^{-1}) and rebounds with a speed of 11 m s^{-1} (velocity 11 m s^{-1}).

(c)

(d) When $t = 1$, ball's speed $= 10 \text{ m s}^{-1}$

C Change in velocity (p. 46)

1D (a) *Car A*
The car moves 30 cm every second, relative to the mat, while the mat is simultaneously moving 40 cm every second in the same direction.

Hence the velocity of car A is $(40 + 30) \text{ cm s}^{-1} = 70 \text{ cm s}^{-1}$ in the direction of the motion of the mat.

Car B
The car moves 30 cm every second, relative to the mat, in a direction opposite to that of the motion of the

mat. The mat is simultaneously moving 40 cm every second.

Hence the velocity of car B is $(40-30) \text{ cm s}^{-1} = 10 \text{ cm s}^{-1}$ in the direction of the motion of the mat.

Car C
Every second the car moves 30 cm relative to the mat, perpendicular to the direction of the motion of the mat. The mat is simultaneously moving 40 cm every second.

The magnitude of the velocity of car C is 50 cm s^{-1}.

$\tan \theta = \frac{30}{40} \implies \theta \approx 36.9°$

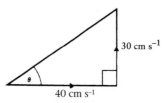

That is, the velocity of car C is 50 cm s^{-1} making an angle of $36.9°$ with the direction of the motion of the mat.

(b) The change in velocity for each car is 40 cm s^{-1} in the direction of motion of the mat.

(c) In each case,

Initial velocity + Change in velocity
= Final velocity

For example, for car A

	Change		Initial
	40		30
		Final	
		70	

Exercise C (p. 48)

1 (a) 13 m s^{-1} due west
(b) 13 m s^{-1} due east
(c)

$\sqrt{8^2 + 5^2} = 9.43$ (to 3 s.f.)

$\tan \alpha = \frac{8}{5} \implies \alpha = 58.0°$

The change in velocity is 9.43 m s^{-1} in direction $328°$.

2

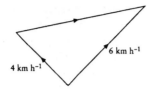

6 km h⁻¹

4 km h⁻¹

The change in velocity is 7.2 km h^{-1} in direction 079°.

3   Resultant velocity of aeroplane

$$= \begin{bmatrix} 200 \\ 10 \end{bmatrix} + \begin{bmatrix} -30 \\ 40 \end{bmatrix} \text{km h}^{-1}$$

$$= \begin{bmatrix} 170 \\ 50 \end{bmatrix} \text{km h}^{-1}$$

The resultant velocity of the aeroplane is 177.2 km h^{-1} in direction 073.6°.

4   Change in velocity $= \begin{bmatrix} 6 \\ 6 \end{bmatrix} \text{m s}^{-1}$

Its magnitude is 8.5 m s^{-1}. Its direction is 045°.

5   Velocity of the wind ≈ 14.0 km h^{-1} in direction 142°.

D   Resultant velocity (p. 48)

1   (a)   Place the point of your compass at the right hand end of the current vector and draw an arc of radius 4 units to intersect the resultant velocity vector.

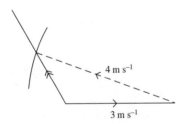

4 m s⁻¹

3 m s⁻¹

(b)   It is difficult because there is no fixed point to which the canoe should be pointing.

(c)   From the drawing (or trigonometry), the resultant velocity has magnitude 1.5 m s^{-1}.

The journey time from A to B is $\frac{100}{1.5} = 66.7$ seconds.

The time from B to C is the same.

The time from C to A is $\frac{100}{7} = 14.3$ seconds.

The total journey time is about $66.7 + 66.7 + 14.3 = 147.7$ seconds.

This should be rounded to 150 seconds.

Exercise D (p. 51)

1   By Pythagoras's theorem, her speed is

$\sqrt{8^2 + 2^2} = 8.25$ m s^{-1} (to 3 s.f.)

2 $\cos \theta \approx \frac{1}{1.5} \Rightarrow \theta \approx 48°$

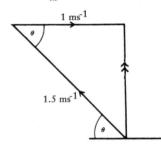

1 ms⁻¹

θ

1.5 ms⁻¹

θ

The girl should point her canoe upriver making an angle of 48° with the bank.

Resultant speed $= 1.1$ m s^{-1}

Time taken to cross river

$$= \frac{100}{\text{Resultant speed}}$$

≈ 89 seconds

Assumptions made:

● She can paddle immediately with speed 1.5 m s^{-1}.

● She can maintain both this speed and the direction throughout the motion.

● The speed of the river is the same throughout its width.

3   75 m;   25 seconds

4   You should point the canoe into the current at an angle of 41.4° to the bank. It will take 38 seconds to cross.

5   Like other questions in the exercise, this can be tackled by writing the vectors in component form.

$$V_{\text{canoe}} = \begin{bmatrix} -4 \cos 45° \\ 4 \sin 45° \end{bmatrix} \qquad V_{\text{river}} = \begin{bmatrix} 3 \\ 0 \end{bmatrix}$$

$$V_{\text{resultant}} = \begin{bmatrix} -4 \cos 45° \\ 4 \sin 45° \end{bmatrix} + \begin{bmatrix} 3 \\ 0 \end{bmatrix} = \begin{bmatrix} -0.17 \\ 2.83 \end{bmatrix}$$

The canoe takes $\frac{100}{2.83} = 35$ s to cross the river.

It will end up 6.1 m upstream on the other bank.

6   Sketch

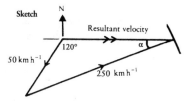

The wind blows at 50 km h^{-1} from a bearing of 030°. Draw this vector first.

The plane flies at a speed of 250 km h^{-1} but you do not know its direction. Draw a circular arc of radius 250.

The resultant must be due east. Draw a vector from the start due east. This completes your vector triangle.

Scale drawing   *Scale* **1 cm : 50 km h^{-1}**

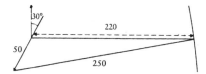

By measurement, the resultant velocity is about 220 km h^{-1} due east. The plane must head on a bearing of 080°.

The plane must cover 100 km, so the time taken is $\frac{100}{220} = 0.4545$ hour.

This is approximately 27 minutes.

Notice that the sine rule applied to the first triangle gives

$$\sin \alpha = \frac{50 \sin 120°}{250}$$

$\alpha = 9.97°$, confirming the bearing.

7E   He should swim at an angle of 48° to the bank. The resultant speed will be 3.7 km h^{-1}.

E   A modelling exercise (p. 52)

1   The various factors to consider are:
(a) the velocity of the plane
(b) the wind velocity
(c) the altitude.

Assume that the velocity of the plane is constant and ignore the acceleration and retardation of starting and stopping. A speed of 150 m s^{-1} is reasonable for a light aircraft.

You may find it helpful to assume that the wind velocity is zero, in a preliminary calculation. Ignore the variation of fuel consumption with altitude. It is probably not significant for a light aircraft which will not fly very high.

Model 1
Let the wind velocity be zero and the plane have velocity 150 m s^{-1}.

Travelling at 150 m s^{-1} north for 2 hours gives a maximum distance from the base of $(150 \times 3600 \times 2)$ m = 1080 km.

Model 2
Now let the velocity of the wind be 30 m s^{-1} south. Suppose that d metres is the maximum possible distance from base.

Outward journey   Homeward journey

On the outward journey the resultant speed is 120 m s^{-1} and the time taken is $d \div 120$ seconds.

On the homeward journey the resultant speed is 180 m s^{-1} and the time taken is $d \div 180$ seconds.

The total time must be 4 hours, so

$$\frac{d}{120} + \frac{d}{180} = 14\,400$$

$$\Rightarrow d = 1\,036\,800 \text{ (metres)}$$

The maximum distance that you can fly from base and return safely is 1036 km.

Model 3
Now generalise a little by letting the wind speed be v m s^{-1} south.

The resultant speed out is $(150 - v)$ m s^{-1}.
The resultant speed back is
$(150 + v)$ m s^{-1}.

$$\frac{d}{150 - v} + \frac{d}{150 + v} = 14\,400$$

$$\Rightarrow d = 48(150^2 - v^2)$$

Drawing a graph of v against d gives

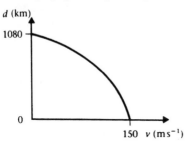

When $v = 0$, then $d = 1080$ as in model 1.

The value of d is not altered if v is replaced by $-v$. Thus the result is the same whether the wind blows south or north. (Sketch the appropriate graph.)

If the velocity is greater than 150 m s^{-1} then d is negative and the aeroplane can never return to base!

As v increases then d decreases slowly at first and then more rapidly.

5 Changes in motion

A Momentum – the 'quantity of motion' (p. 53)

1D The answers are given in the paragraphs which follow the questions.

2D The answers are given in the paragraphs which follow the questions.

3 (a) The faster the snooker ball is rolled, the harder it is to stop and the more effect it has on the block which it hits.

   (b) This also occurs with the table tennis ball.

(c) However, at any given speed, the table tennis ball is much easier to stop than the snooker ball and has much less effect on the block.

4 (a), (b) You should be able to feel a definite difference in the effort needed to stop the balls as they fall further. The further they fall the greater their velocity.

(c) As a result of the experiments, the important factors of the quantity of motion are seen to be the mass and the velocity of the moving object.

A reasonable way of combining these would be by multiplying the two together, since the quantity of motion appears to increase with both mass and velocity.

5 If mass and velocity are multiplied for the lorry, the quantity of motion would be 4000×1 kg m s^{-1}. For the car the quantity of motion is $800 \times 5 = 4000$ kg m s^{-1}.

Thus the car and the lorry would have the same quantity of motion.

6 A rough idea of speeds can be gained without any detailed measurement or timing, although a ruler and watch can be used to improve accuracy a little. There is no need for more sophisticated timing methods in these experiments.

Initially random selections of masses can be made. After a few attempts, the outcome of an experiment should be predicted *before* the experiment is performed. Conclusions can then be confirmed with a systematic choice of masses.

Results can be recorded easily in a simple table of possibilities and outcomes.

(a) When the two trucks are of equal mass, the moving one will stop and the initially stationary truck will move away. The speed with which the trucks separate can be seen to be roughly equal to the speed of approach.

When the moving truck is more massive than the stationary one, the moving truck will have its speed reduced and the initially stationary truck will move away with a greater speed than the initial speed of approach. The speed with which the trucks separate is again equal to the speed of approach, although this result may not be as apparent as in the case when the masses are equal.

When the moving truck is less massive than the stationary one, the trucks will move off in opposite directions after the collision. The direction of motion of the initially moving truck will therefore be reversed. The speed of separation is again roughly equal to the speed of approach.

(b) When the trucks have equal mass, it can be observed that the resultant speed of the joined trucks is roughly half of the moving truck's original speed. In general, if the two trucks have masses a and b then the resultant speed of the joined trucks is $\dfrac{a}{a+b}$ of the original speed of the moving truck of mass a, although this will be difficult to observe.

Exercise A (p. 56)

1 (b) and (c) have the same momentum, which is 15 kg m s^{-1} eastwards. (a) is in a different direction.

2 $70 \times \begin{bmatrix} 3 \\ 4 \end{bmatrix} = \begin{bmatrix} 210 \\ 280 \end{bmatrix}$ kg m s^{-1}

which has magnitude

$70 \times \sqrt{3^2 + 4^2} = 70 \times 5 = 350$ kg m s^{-1}

in the direction making angle $\tan^{-1} \frac{3}{4}$ with north, i.e. bearing 037°.

3 (a)

The car has three times the speed of the truck but only one tenth of its mass.

(b)

The speedboat has a greater speed than the ferry but a much smaller mass.

(c) 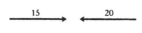 The jeep is slightly faster than the rhino but the rhino is slightly heavier.

B Conservation of momentum (p. 57)

Exercise B (p. 60)

1 (a)

Momentum before   Momentum after

————→ 20   ←———— 10v

$20 = 10v \implies v = 2$

The velocity of B has magnitude of 2 m s^{-1}.

(b)   Momentum before

————→ 15   ←———— 20

Momentum after

←———— 10   ————→ 10v

$15 - 20 = 10v - 10 \implies v = \frac{1}{2}$

The velocity of B has magnitude $\frac{1}{2}$ m s^{-1}.

(c)

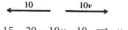

15v 15

20

$15v = \sqrt{15^2 + 20^2} \implies v = 1\frac{2}{3}$

This is a velocity of $1\frac{2}{3}$ m s^{-1} at an angle of $\tan^{-1} \frac{3}{4}$ to the original direction of the motion of A.

2 19 m s^{-1} (to 2 s.f.)

3 3 m s^{-1}

4 2 kg

5

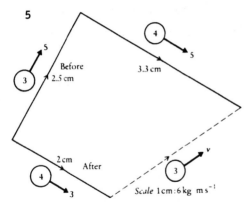

The final velocity of the 3 kg mass is $\frac{17}{3} \approx 5.7$ m s^{-1} on bearing 058°.

6   0.46 m s^{-1} at 16° to the original direction of motion.

C   Change in momentum (p. 61)

1D   Loss of momentum = $60 \times 5 - 60 \times 4.2$
$= 48$ kg m s^{-1},

equal to the amount gained by Louise since the total momentum is unchanged.

2   (a)   Once the ball is in motion on a horizontal surface it will be moving in a straight line with constant speed. On applying the blow at 90° to this straight line, the ball will be deflected at an angle to the original direction of motion and will continue to move in a straight line in the new direction, with a new speed.

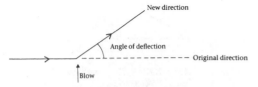

Varying the strength of the blow will vary the angle of deflection, the angle increasing as the strength of the blow increases.

(b)   If the blow is kept as constant as possible, it should be observed that the heavier balls are deflected less than the lighter ones.

(c)   The paths of the two balls are shown below.

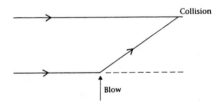

The ball that receives the blow should keep level with the other ball in the original direction of motion.

This shows that the blow, when applied at right angles to the original motion, does not affect the original motion along the horizontal surface. The blow gives the ball a component of velocity at right angles to its original direction while leaving the original component unchanged.

To summarise:

● If the mass is fixed, the change in velocity caused by the blow increases as the blow increases.

● If the blow is fixed, the change in velocity decreases as the mass increases.

● The blow changes the velocity in the direction of the blow.

Thus the blow changes the momentum in the direction of the blow. The change in momentum increases as the blow increases.

Exercise C (p. 62)

1   The speed increases from 18.05 m s^{-1} to 33.3 m s^{-1}. The initial momentum is 180 556 kg m s^{-1} and the final momentum is 333 333 kg m s^{-1}.

The change in momentum is 152 777 kg m s^{-1}
$= 153\,000$ kg m s^{-1} to 3 significant figures.

2   (a)   Initial momentum = 30 000 kg m s^{-1}
New momentum = 15 000 kg m s^{-1}
The new speed is 7.5 m s^{-1}.

(b)   Initial momentum = 150 000 kg m s^{-1}
New momentum = 135 000 kg m s^{-1}
The new speed is 13.5 m s^{-1}.

3   Momentum before = $\begin{bmatrix} 2.5 \\ 0.2 \end{bmatrix}$ kg m s^{-1}

Momentum after = $\begin{bmatrix} -1.5 \\ 0.5 \end{bmatrix}$ kg m s^{-1}

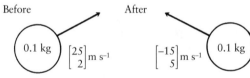

Before   After

0.1 kg $\begin{bmatrix} 25 \\ 2 \end{bmatrix}$ m s^{-1} $\begin{bmatrix} -15 \\ 5 \end{bmatrix}$ m s^{-1} 0.1 kg

(a)   The impulse is $\begin{bmatrix} -4.0 \\ 0.3 \end{bmatrix}$ kg m s^{-1}.

(b)   If the impulse is $\begin{bmatrix} -2.0 \\ 0.15 \end{bmatrix}$ kg m s^{-1}, then

the new momentum is $\begin{bmatrix} 0.5 \\ 0.35 \end{bmatrix}$ m s^{-1}.

The new velocity would be $\begin{bmatrix} 5 \\ 3.5 \end{bmatrix}$ m s^{-1}.

6   Force

A   Newton's first and second laws of motion (p. 64)

1   (a)   Your graph should have the general shape of the graph shown.

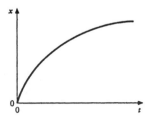

(b)   Your results will only be approximate but should show that the velocity decreases by about 40 cm s^{-1} every second.

Exercise A (p. 66)

1 $m\mathbf{u} + \mathbf{F}t = m\mathbf{v}$, $\mathbf{F} = 20$ N in the direction of motion, $m = 2$ kg

$t = 0, u = 0$ $2 \times 0 + 20 \times 1 = 2v$

$t = 1, v = ?$ $\Rightarrow v = 10$ m s^{-1}

$t = 2,$ $v = 20$ m s^{-1}

$t = 3,$ $v = 30$ m s^{-1}

$t = 4,$ $v = 40$ m s^{-1}

The speed is increased by a constant amount each second.

2 $m\mathbf{u} + \mathbf{F}t = m\mathbf{v}$ $t = 5,$ $m = 0.2,$
take north as positive.

$0.2 \times (-1.5) + F \times 5 = 0.2 \times 2$

$\Rightarrow$ $F = 0.14$

A force of 0.14 N is needed, acting due north.

3   The time taken is 4.8 seconds.

4   A force of 5250 N is required.

5   The speed is 2.25 m s^{-1}.

B   Newton's third law (p. 67)

1D   The skateboard experiment may be carried out practically. Subject to effects such as differences in the two skateboards themselves, you could expect:

(a)   the interaction forces of the two students to be equal in magnitude and opposite in direction

(b)   their momenta to be equal in magnitude and opposite in direction, at least initially.

The two students still exert the same force on each other, even if one is twice the weight of the other. Because their momenta are the same in magnitude, the heavier student will move off with half the speed of the lighter. (Note that if two skateboarders have a rope, they can pull towards one another in the same manner.)

Exercise B (p. 68)

1   The weight of the apple is the gravitational force due to the attraction of the Earth. Thus the 'other body' is the Earth. The total momentum of the Earth and the apple is conserved. This implies that the Earth moves towards the apple as well as the apple moving towards the Earth. This does, in fact, happen but the mass of the Earth is so much greater than that of the apple that the effect is far too small to measure.

2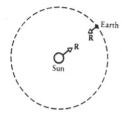

There is a gravitational force exerted by the Sun on the Earth and a force, equal in magnitude and opposite in direction, exerted by the Earth on the Sun. Once again, the total momentum of the system is conserved.

However, the mass of the Sun is far greater than that of the Earth and so the effect on the Earth's velocity is much greater than the effect on the velocity of the Sun.

The pull of the Sun causes a change in the Earth's velocity but not its speed. This motion must, of course, satisfy Newton's second law.

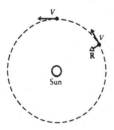

C   Weight and change of momentum
(p. 68)

1D   (a)   A set of scales registers the same weight for the golf ball no matter at what height it is used. The pull on the golf ball is therefore the same throughout its motion and so its momentum changes at a constant rate. The (time, velocity) graph will therefore be linear.

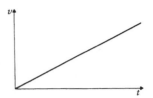

(b)   Contrary to what many people believe, the speed at which an object falls does not depend upon its mass. (You may have seen a film of the experiment performed on the Moon where in the absence of air resistance a feather falls at the same rate as a stone.) Air resistance has a negligible effect on the golf and cricket balls and so they have the same speed at any time.

Since the balls have the same speed at any time their changes in momenta are in proportion to their masses. By Newton's second law, the resultant forces acting on them must be in proportion to their masses. The weight of an object is therefore a fixed multiple of its mass.

2   (a)   The velocity can be found by estimating the gradient of the (time, displacement) graph. Your estimates should be close to those shown in the table below.

Time t (seconds)	0	0.5	1.0	1.5	2.0
Velocity v (m s^{-1})	0	−5	−10	−15	−20

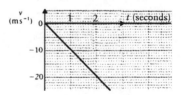

The (time, velocity) graph is shown above. The linear relationship shows that the magnitude of the velocity (the speed) is increasing at a steady 10 m s^{-1} each second. The velocity is negative because the direction is downwards.

(b) During the first second the momentum of the shot changes from 0 to −10 kg m s⁻¹, and during the next second the momentum changes from −10 to −20 kg m s⁻¹. The change in momentum is therefore −10 kg m s⁻¹ during each second.

(c) You should expect the change in momentum to continue to be −10 kg m s⁻¹ per second.

(d) According to Newton's second law the change in momentum each second is a measure of the resultant force acting on the shot, so it would seem that there is a constant force of −10 newtons pulling the shot down. (The force is negative simply because it is acting in what has been taken to be the negative direction.) This is clearly the force of gravitational attraction.

It is interesting to note that if a second shot with a mass of 0.5 kg had been released simultaneously with the 1 kg shot, it would have had the same velocity and so its change in momentum would only have been −5 kg m s⁻¹ per second. The force of gravitational attraction on a 0.5 kg mass would therefore be −5 N. The force of gravitational attraction would appear to be a constant −10 N per kilogram.

3 (a)

Time	Velocity
1	$\begin{bmatrix} 10 \\ 20 \end{bmatrix}$
2	$\begin{bmatrix} 10 \\ 10 \end{bmatrix}$
3	$\begin{bmatrix} 10 \\ 0 \end{bmatrix}$
4	$\begin{bmatrix} 10 \\ -10 \end{bmatrix}$
5	$\begin{bmatrix} 10 \\ -20 \end{bmatrix}$

(b)

The velocity can be expressed as a column vector.

(c) The tip of each momentum vector lies on the same vertical line. Therefore the horizontal component of momentum is the same in each case, and so the speed of the ball along the horizontal direction remains constant.

The change in momentum in each second is in the downward vertical direction.

Change in momentum during the 2nd second is 1 kg m s⁻¹.

Change in momentum during the 3rd second is 1 kg m s⁻¹.

Change in momentum during the 4th second is 1 kg m s⁻¹.

Change in momentum during the 5th second is 1 kg m s⁻¹.

(d) The change in momentum during each second is the same; 1 kg m s⁻¹ downwards. The same constant rate of change of momentum is seen when a ball (or an apple) falls vertically downwards. It is caused by its weight, i.e. the force due to the gravitational attraction of the Earth.

Exercise C (p. 73)

1 (a) When $t = 4$, $v = 39.2$ m s⁻¹
(b) The distance fallen is the area under the graph, 78.4 metres.
(c) The cliff is 99 metres high.

2 (a)

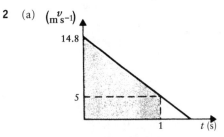

(b) The graph shows that after 1 second the ball will have slowed to 5 m s⁻¹.

The distance travelled is given by the area under the graph $s = 9.9$ metres. The highest conker can be 9.9 metres above the ground.

3 (a)

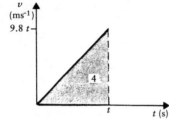

(b) $4 = \dfrac{9.8t \times t}{2} \implies t = 0.90$ seconds.

The velocity with which the tin hits the ground is 8.9 m s^{-1}.

4 $s = 0.5gt^2$ so $t = 1.01$ seconds

Both have a velocity of 9.9 m s^{-1}. The girl has momentum of 247 kg m s^{-1} and her father has momentum of 742 kg m s^{-1}.

5 The momentum is 16 000 kg m s^{-1} so the velocity is 8 m s^{-1}.

$t = 8 \div 9.8 = 0.82$ seconds

Then $s = 0.5 \times 8 \times 0.82 = 3.3$ metres.

7 More kinematics

A Acceleration (p. 75)

1D To a non-mathematician, acceleration is understood as rate of change of speed. The mathematical definition is rate of change of velocity, a vector which need not even be in the direction of motion (see, for example, Chapter 6, Section C). For straight line motion always in the same direction, the two ideas give the same value.

2 (a) The gradient of a velocity–time graph is the acceleration.

(b) $a = $ gradient BC $= \dfrac{v - u}{t} \implies v = u + at$

(c) $s = $ area OABC $= \frac{1}{2}(u + v)t$

(d) (i) $s = \frac{1}{2}(u + u + at)t = ut + \frac{1}{2}at^2$

(ii) $ut = $ area of the rectangle with OA and OC as sides. The rest of the trapezium OAEC is a triangle with base t and height at; the area is $\frac{1}{2}at^2$.

(e) $s = \frac{1}{2}(u + v)t$

$= \frac{1}{2}(u + v) \times \dfrac{v - u}{a} = \dfrac{v^2 - u^2}{2a}$.

Hence $v^2 = u^2 + 2as$.

Exercise A (p. 77)

1 $s = ut + \frac{1}{2}at^2$ gives $s = 440$.

$v = u + at$ gives $v = 30$.

The distance is 440 m and speed 30 m s^{-1}.

2 2.38 m s^{-2}, 189 m

3 $v^2 = u^2 + 2as$, gives $a = -1.72$.

The time is 12.2 s.

4 7.81 m, 6.25 s

5 $v^2 = 12^2 - 2 \times 10 \times 5$, taking $g = -10$ m s^{-2}.

$v = \pm 6.63,\ t = \dfrac{12 - 6.63}{10}$ or $\dfrac{12 + 6.63}{10}$

$= 0.54$ or 1.86

6 (a) $a = \dfrac{1.8^2}{6.4}$, $v^2 = u^2 + 2as$ now gives

$v^2 = 1.8^2 - \frac{1}{2} \times 1.8^2$, so $v = 1.27$.

(b) Velocity at the halfway point is

$\dfrac{u}{\sqrt{2}}$ m s^{-1}.

B Variable acceleration in straight-line motion (p. 78)

1 $a = t + 1$ $v = \frac{1}{2}t^2 + t + 3$

$y = \frac{1}{6}t^3 + \frac{1}{2}t^2 + 3t + 2$

When $t = 1$, $a = 2$, $v = 4.5$ and $y = 5\frac{2}{3}$

Exercise B (p. 80)

1 $v = 4t^3 + 2t = 36$ when $t = 2$

$a = 12t^2 + 2 = 50$ when $t = 2$

2 $v = \frac{1}{3}t^3 - \frac{1}{2}t^2 + t + 2 = 2\frac{5}{6}$ when $t = 1$

$x = \frac{1}{12}t^4 - \frac{1}{6}t^3 + \frac{1}{2}t^2 + 2t + 3 = 5\frac{5}{12}$ when $t = 1$

3 $x = t^3 + t^2 + 4t + 1$, $a = 6t + 2$

4 $v = 10t + 8$, $x = 5t^2 + 8t$

When $x = 22$, $5t^2 + 8t - 22 = 0$,

$t = 1.44$ (or -3.04),

$v = 22.4$ (or -22.4)

5 $\dfrac{dv}{dt} = a \implies v = at + u$ if $v = u$ when $t = 0$

$\implies s = \frac{1}{2}at^2 + ut$ if $s = 0$ when $t = 0$

C Motion in two dimensions (p. 80)

1 $\begin{bmatrix} x \\ y \end{bmatrix} = \begin{bmatrix} 6t \\ 9t - 5t^2 \end{bmatrix}$

2 (a) $\mathbf{v} = \dfrac{d\mathbf{r}}{dt}$ and for small δt, $\delta\mathbf{r} = \begin{bmatrix} \delta x \\ \delta y \end{bmatrix}$,

so $\dfrac{d\mathbf{r}}{dt} = \begin{bmatrix} \dfrac{dx}{dt} \\ \dfrac{dy}{dt} \end{bmatrix}$

(b) If $\mathbf{r} = \begin{bmatrix} 6t \\ 9t - 5t^2 \end{bmatrix}$, $\mathbf{v} = \begin{bmatrix} 6 \\ 9 - 10t \end{bmatrix}$

(c) $t = 0.7$, $\mathbf{v} = \begin{bmatrix} 6 \\ 2 \end{bmatrix}$; $t = 0.9$, $\mathbf{v} = \begin{bmatrix} 6 \\ 0 \end{bmatrix}$;

$t = 1.1$, $\mathbf{v} = \begin{bmatrix} 6 \\ -2 \end{bmatrix}$

(d) The ball lands when $t = 1.8$ and

$\mathbf{v} = \begin{bmatrix} 6 \\ -9 \end{bmatrix}$, so its speed is

$\sqrt{6^2 + 9^2} = 10.8$ m s^{-1}.

(e) This can be interpreted as follows.

The starting speed and landing speed are the same. The horizontal component of velocity is always the same, but the vertical component is steadily decreasing from 9 m s^{-1} on take-off to zero after 0.9 seconds, to -9 m s^{-1} on landing.

In the absence of any real data on speeds and velocities these results are validated simply by common sense. You can expect the vertical component of velocity to decrease because of the weight. The effect of air resistance seems to have been negligible in the 1.8 seconds of the flight. However, the actual motion could be studied on a video, frame by frame.

Exercise C (p. 83)

1 If $\mathbf{r} = \begin{bmatrix} 10t \\ 30t - 5t^2 \end{bmatrix}$ then $\mathbf{v} = \begin{bmatrix} 10 \\ 30 - 10t \end{bmatrix}$

(a) $\dfrac{dy}{dt} = 0$ when $t = 3$

(b) When $t = 3$, $\mathbf{v} = \begin{bmatrix} 10 \\ 0 \end{bmatrix}$ and $\mathbf{r} = \begin{bmatrix} 30 \\ 45 \end{bmatrix}$

so the maximum height = 45 metres

(c) When $t = 6$, $\mathbf{r} = \begin{bmatrix} 60 \\ 0 \end{bmatrix}$

so the range = 60 metres

2 (a) At $t = 0$, $\mathbf{v} = \begin{bmatrix} 6 \\ 9 \end{bmatrix}$

so speed $= \sqrt{6^2 + 9^2} = 10.8$ m s^{-1}

(b) When $t = 0.9$, $\mathbf{v} = \begin{bmatrix} 6 \\ 0 \end{bmatrix}$

so speed = 6 m s^{-1}

3 (a) Height = 3 m when $t = 0$ or

$t = \dfrac{11}{5} = 2.2$.

When $t = 2.2$, $\mathbf{r} = \begin{bmatrix} 44 \\ 3 \end{bmatrix}$; the net should

be 44 m from the starting point.

(b) $\mathbf{v} = \begin{bmatrix} 20 \\ 11 - 10t \end{bmatrix} = \begin{bmatrix} 20 \\ 11 \end{bmatrix}$ when $t = 0$

and $\begin{bmatrix} 20 \\ -11 \end{bmatrix}$ when $t = 2.2$.

Landing speed = 22.8 m s^{-1}.

4 $\mathbf{r} = \begin{bmatrix} 10t \\ 2 + 10t - 5t^2 \end{bmatrix}$

(a) $\dfrac{d\mathbf{r}}{dt} = \begin{bmatrix} 10 \\ 10 - 10t \end{bmatrix}$

$\Rightarrow$ velocity of projection $= \begin{bmatrix} 10 \\ 10 \end{bmatrix}$

$\Rightarrow$ magnitude $= 10\sqrt{2}$ m s^{-1},
direction = 45° to the horizontal

(b) $t = 0$, $\mathbf{r} = \begin{bmatrix} 0 \\ 2 \end{bmatrix}$

The height of release above ground is 2 metres.

(c) The shot hits the ground when

$2 + 10t - 5t^2 = 0$

i.e. $t = 2.18$ seconds (to 2 d.p.)
Distance thrown = 21.8 m

(d) $\dfrac{d\mathbf{r}}{dt} = \begin{bmatrix} 10 \\ 10 - 10t \end{bmatrix} = \begin{bmatrix} 10 \\ -11.8 \end{bmatrix}$

on striking the ground.

(e) It is moving horizontally when
$10 - 10t = 0$

It moves horizontally when
$t = 1$ second.
It is then at its maximum height.

(f) Height $= 2 + 10t - 5t^2 = 7$ m when
$t = 1$

5 $\mathbf{r} = \begin{bmatrix} 0.5 + 10t \\ 0.75 + 2.8t - 5t^2 \end{bmatrix}$

(a) Initial velocity $= \begin{bmatrix} 10 \\ 2.8 \end{bmatrix}$ m s^{-1}

(b) $t = 0$ on take-off, $\mathbf{r} = \begin{bmatrix} 0.5 \\ 0.75 \end{bmatrix}$ metres

i.e. the centre of gravity is in front of the take-off board.

(c) On landing, $0.75 + 2.8t - 5t^2 = 0.75$
$\Rightarrow t(2.8 - 5t) = 0$

$\Rightarrow t = 0$ or $t = \dfrac{2.8}{5} = 0.56$ seconds

Length of jump
$= 0.5 + 10 \times 0.56$ seconds
$= 6.1$ metres

(d) The question treats the jumper as a particle. The motion of the centre of gravity cannot be controlled after take-off.

D   Newton's second law, re-phrased
(p. 85)

1D $\mathbf{F} = \dfrac{d}{dt}(m\mathbf{v}) = m\dfrac{d}{dt}(\mathbf{v}) = m\mathbf{a}$

Exercise D (p. 86)

1 $\mathbf{v} = \begin{bmatrix} 9 - 2t \\ 9 - 2t \end{bmatrix}$ m s^{-1}

$\mathbf{a} = \begin{bmatrix} -2 \\ -2 \end{bmatrix}$ m s^{-2}

$\mathbf{F} = m\mathbf{a} \Rightarrow \mathbf{F} = \begin{bmatrix} -0.2 \\ -0.2 \end{bmatrix}$ newtons

2 $\mathbf{v} = \begin{bmatrix} 5 - 2t \\ 5 - 2t \end{bmatrix}$

$\mathbf{a} = \begin{bmatrix} -2 \\ -2 \end{bmatrix}$

$\Rightarrow \mathbf{F} = m\mathbf{a} = 70\begin{bmatrix} -2 \\ -2 \end{bmatrix} = \begin{bmatrix} -140 \\ -140 \end{bmatrix}$ N

3 $\mathbf{v} = \begin{bmatrix} 6t \\ 8t \end{bmatrix}$ $\mathbf{a} = \begin{bmatrix} 6 \\ 8 \end{bmatrix}$

$\Rightarrow \mathbf{F} = 0.5\begin{bmatrix} 6 \\ 8 \end{bmatrix} = \begin{bmatrix} 3 \\ 4 \end{bmatrix}$

$\Rightarrow F = 5$ N at an angle $\tan^{-1}\frac{4}{3}$ to the x-axis

4 $\mathbf{a} = \begin{bmatrix} 0 \\ 2t \end{bmatrix}$, $\mathbf{v} = \begin{bmatrix} 3 \\ t^2 \end{bmatrix}$, $\mathbf{r} = \begin{bmatrix} 3t \\ \frac{1}{3}t^3 \end{bmatrix}$

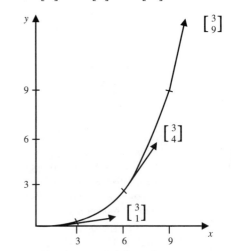

5 $\mathbf{a} = \begin{bmatrix} -3t \\ 2 \end{bmatrix}$, $\mathbf{v} = \begin{bmatrix} -\frac{3}{2}t^2 + 20 \\ 2t + 4 \end{bmatrix}$,

$\mathbf{r} = \begin{bmatrix} -\frac{1}{2}t^3 + 20t \\ t^2 + 4t \end{bmatrix}$

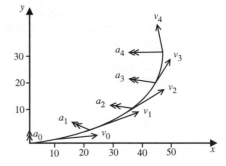

6 $\quad \mathbf{a} = \begin{bmatrix} 12t - 2 \\ 2 \end{bmatrix}, \quad \mathbf{r} = \begin{bmatrix} 2t^3 - t^2 + 4 \\ t^2 + 3t - 1 \end{bmatrix}$

8 Projectile motion

A Motion under gravity (p. 88)

1 Stones, snowballs, hockey balls, cricket balls thrown from the outfield, basketballs are examples where the paths are roughly parabolic and lie in a vertical plane. It is reasonable to treat their flights as projectile motion.

In golf, football and rugby, wind and spin often affect the motion. Polishing half of a cricket ball can accentuate swing when it is bowled. The mathematics of this chapter is not applicable to these situations.

2 Given $\quad \mathbf{v} = \begin{bmatrix} 3.81 \\ 2.2 - 10t \end{bmatrix}$

then $\quad \mathbf{r} = \begin{bmatrix} 3.81t + c_1 \\ 2.2t - 5t^2 + c_2 \end{bmatrix}$

When $t = 0$, $\mathbf{r} = \begin{bmatrix} 0 \\ 0 \end{bmatrix} \Rightarrow c_1 = c_2 = 0$

So $\quad \mathbf{r} = \begin{bmatrix} 3.81t \\ 2.2t - 5t^2 \end{bmatrix}$

3 (a) $(2.2 - 5t)t = 0$

$\Rightarrow t = 0$ or $t = \dfrac{2.2}{5} = 0.44$

(b) When $t = 0.44$, $\mathbf{r}(t) = \begin{bmatrix} 3.81 \times 0.44 \\ 0 \end{bmatrix}$

$\approx \begin{bmatrix} 1.7 \\ 0 \end{bmatrix}$

So the range is $R \approx 1.7$ metres.

4 You can conclude that the elastic band will land about 170 cm away, after about 0.44 seconds. During flight its highest point is about 25 cm above the table.

5 It is clear that there is a degree of inaccuracy in these predictions. Problems arise because it is very difficult to measure accurately less than one second even with a stopwatch.

It is possible to measure the range (or even the height) and so validate the theory. Sources of error are

- the point of projection may not be exactly at the end of the table
- the angle of projection may not be exactly 30°
- the velocity of projection will not be exactly 4.4 m s^{-1}
- the elastic band is not a particle.

Exercise A (p. 91)

1 Initial velocity $= \begin{bmatrix} 7 \\ 5 \end{bmatrix}$ m s^{-1}

$\Rightarrow$ displacement $= \begin{bmatrix} 7t \\ 5t - 5t^2 \end{bmatrix}$ metres

The ball is in the air for 1 second. Julian is 7 metres from Ann.

2 $\quad \mathbf{a} = \begin{bmatrix} 0 \\ -g \end{bmatrix} = \begin{bmatrix} 0 \\ -10 \end{bmatrix}$

$\Rightarrow \mathbf{v} = \begin{bmatrix} 3 \\ 5 - 10t \end{bmatrix}$

$\Rightarrow \mathbf{r} = \begin{bmatrix} 3t \\ 1 + 5t - 5t^2 \end{bmatrix}$

At maximum height, $\quad 5 - 10t = 0$

$\Rightarrow t = 0.5$

Maximum height $= 2.25$ m

3 $\quad \mathbf{a} = \begin{bmatrix} 0 \\ -g \end{bmatrix} = \begin{bmatrix} 0 \\ -10 \end{bmatrix}$

$\mathbf{v} = \begin{bmatrix} 21 \cos 40° \\ 21 \sin 40° - 10t \end{bmatrix} = \begin{bmatrix} 16.1 \\ 13.5 - 10t \end{bmatrix}$

$\mathbf{r} = \begin{bmatrix} 16.1t \\ 2 + 13.5t - 5t^2 \end{bmatrix}$

For length of throw,

$2 + 13.5t - 5t^2 = 0 \Rightarrow t = 2.84$ seconds

The length of the throw is 45.7 m.

4E (a) $\mathbf{v} = \begin{bmatrix} 4 \\ 5 - gt \end{bmatrix} = \begin{bmatrix} 4 \\ 5 - 10t \end{bmatrix}$

$\mathbf{r} = \begin{bmatrix} 4t \\ 5t - 5t^2 \end{bmatrix}$

When $t = 2$, $\mathbf{r} = \begin{bmatrix} 8 \\ -10 \end{bmatrix}$ and the cannon-ball is at A. Furthermore, when $t = 2$, $\mathbf{v} = \begin{bmatrix} 4 \\ -15 \end{bmatrix}$

(b) Let the rebound velocity be **V**. The momentum is conserved.

So $8 \times \begin{bmatrix} 4 \\ -15 \end{bmatrix} = 8 \times \mathbf{V} + 48 \times \begin{bmatrix} 0 \\ -3 \end{bmatrix}$

$\Rightarrow \mathbf{V} = \begin{bmatrix} 4 \\ -15 \end{bmatrix} - 6 \times \begin{bmatrix} 0 \\ -3 \end{bmatrix} = \begin{bmatrix} 4 \\ 3 \end{bmatrix}$

(c) After a further t seconds,

the ball's velocity is $\mathbf{v} = \begin{bmatrix} 4 \\ 3 - 10t \end{bmatrix}$

and $\mathbf{r} = \begin{bmatrix} 8 \\ -10 \end{bmatrix} + \begin{bmatrix} 4t \\ 3t - 5t^2 \end{bmatrix}$

Now $3t - 5t^2 = -2$ when
$5t^2 - 3t - 2 = 0$, i.e. $t = 1$ or -0.4

When $t = 1$, $\mathbf{r} = \begin{bmatrix} 12 \\ -12 \end{bmatrix}$

This takes the cannon-ball clear of the water hazard.

5E (a) $\mathbf{v} = \begin{bmatrix} 3 \\ 4 \\ -10t \end{bmatrix}$

(b) At $t = 0$, $\dot{\mathbf{v}} = \begin{bmatrix} 3 \\ 4 \\ 0 \end{bmatrix}$

There is no upward velocity so the missile travels horizontally at first, on a bearing of 127°.

(d) $10\sqrt{5}$ m   (e) $t = 10\sqrt{6}$ s

(f) $\mathbf{a} = \begin{bmatrix} 0 \\ 0 \\ -10 \end{bmatrix}$ m s^{-2}

Only gravitational force is acting on the rocket, so it is not powered.

B   The general case (p. 93)

Exercise B (p. 94)

1 (a) When $t = \dfrac{2u \sin \phi}{g}$,

$\mathbf{r} = \begin{bmatrix} \dfrac{2u \sin \phi \times u \cos \phi}{g} \\ \dfrac{2u \sin \phi \times u \sin \phi}{g} - \dfrac{g(2u \sin \phi)^2}{2g^2} \end{bmatrix}$

$= \begin{bmatrix} \dfrac{2u^2 \sin \phi \cos \phi}{g} \\ 0 \end{bmatrix} = \begin{bmatrix} \dfrac{u^2 \sin 2\phi}{g} \\ 0 \end{bmatrix}$

(b) When $y = 0$, $x = \dfrac{u^2 \sin 2\phi}{g}$. This is called the range, R. Interpreting this you will find that R increases from 0 to $\dfrac{u^2}{g}$ as ϕ increases from 0° to 45°.

Once ϕ has passed 45° then $\sin 2\phi$ starts to decrease again. Because $\sin 2\phi = \sin 2(90° - \phi)$, the same horizontal distance can be gained by firing either at an angle ϕ or its complementary angle.

The range varies as the square of the velocity for any angle of projection. So if you double the velocity of projection, you multiply the range by 4.

2 (a) $\mathbf{v} = \begin{bmatrix} u \cos \phi \\ u \sin \phi - gt \end{bmatrix}$

At the highest point, $t = \dfrac{u \sin \phi}{g}$,

i.e. $\mathbf{v} = \begin{bmatrix} u \cos \phi \\ 0 \end{bmatrix}$

This is half of the total flight time – the projectile's flight is symmetrical.

(b) $\mathbf{r} = \begin{bmatrix} \dfrac{u^2 \sin 2\phi}{2g} \\ \dfrac{u^2 \sin^2 \phi}{2g} \end{bmatrix}$

and the greatest height reached

$= \dfrac{u^2 \sin^2 \phi}{2g}$

(c) As the speed of projection increases so does the maximum height gained. As the angle of projection increases so does the maximum height gained. This reaches its highest value when the object is thrown vertically upwards.

3 $\dfrac{d\mathbf{v}}{dt} = \mathbf{g} \implies \mathbf{v} = \mathbf{g}t + \mathbf{U}$ by integration

$$\implies \mathbf{r} = \tfrac{1}{2}\mathbf{g}t^2 + \mathbf{U}t$$

The equations are alternative forms of

$$\mathbf{v} = \begin{bmatrix} U_x \\ -gt + U_y \end{bmatrix}, \quad \mathbf{r} = \begin{bmatrix} U_x t \\ -\tfrac{1}{2}gt^2 + U_y t \end{bmatrix}.$$

4 $y = U \sin \phi \times \dfrac{x}{U \cos \phi} - \dfrac{1}{2} g \left(\dfrac{x}{U \cos \phi} \right)^2$

$= qx - px^2$

where $q = \dfrac{\sin \phi}{\cos \phi} = \tan \phi$, $p = \dfrac{g}{2U^2 \cos^2 \phi}$

5 They all land on the floor at the same time. In fact they always have the same height. The range increases as the horizontal speed of projection is increased.

6 $\mathbf{v} = \begin{bmatrix} 15 \\ 20 - 10t \end{bmatrix}$ $\mathbf{r} = \begin{bmatrix} 15t \\ 20t - 5t^2 \end{bmatrix}$

(a) When $t = 2$, $\mathbf{v} = \begin{bmatrix} 15 \\ 0 \end{bmatrix}$ and

$\mathbf{r} = \begin{bmatrix} 30 \\ 20 \end{bmatrix}$ so it rises to a height of

20 metres.

(b) When $t = 4$, $\mathbf{r} = \begin{bmatrix} 60 \\ 0 \end{bmatrix}$ and it bounces

60 m away.

7

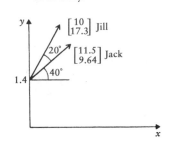

Jill's stone has velocity and displacement

$$\mathbf{v} = \begin{bmatrix} 10 \\ 17.3 - 10t \end{bmatrix}$$

$$\mathbf{r} = \begin{bmatrix} 10t \\ 17.3t - 5t^2 + 1.4 \end{bmatrix}$$

Jack's stone has velocity and displacement

$$\mathbf{v} = \begin{bmatrix} 11.5 \\ 9.64 - 10t \end{bmatrix}$$

$$\mathbf{r} = \begin{bmatrix} 11.5t \\ 9.64t - 5t^2 + 1.4 \end{bmatrix}$$

(a) When Jill's stone is at its highest point,

$$\mathbf{v} = \begin{bmatrix} 10 \\ 0 \end{bmatrix} \implies t = 1.73$$

Her stone rises to $t(17.3 - 5t) + 1.4$ $= 16.4$ metres.

(b) Jill: Her stone lands when
$1.4 + 17.3t - 5t^2 = 0$
$t = 3.54$ or -0.08 so Jill's stone lands after 3.54 seconds.

Jack: His stone lands when
$1.4 + 9.64t - 5t^2 = 0$
$t = 2.06$ or -0.13 so his stone lands after 2.06 seconds.

Jack's stone lands first.

(c) Jill: Horizontal distance
$= 10t = 35.4$ metres

Jack: Horizontal distance
$= 11.5t = 23.7$ metres

Jill's stone lands further away.

8 (a) Set up the model:
Ignore air resistance.
Let the trees be d metres away.

Analysis:
The velocity of the package is

$$\begin{bmatrix} 30 \\ -10t \end{bmatrix} \text{ m s}^{-1}$$

so $\begin{bmatrix} x \\ y \end{bmatrix} = \begin{bmatrix} 30t \\ 210 - 5t^2 \end{bmatrix}$

After T seconds $30T = d$ and
$210 - 5T^2 = 30$
$T = 6$ and $d = 180$

(b) Let the package land D metres from the release point after T seconds.
Then $30T = D$ and $210 - 5T^2 = 0$
$T \approx 6.48$ and $D = 194.4$
The package lands 14.4 metres beyond the trees.

9   The initial velocity is $\begin{bmatrix} 16 \\ 24.5 \end{bmatrix}$ m s^{-1}.

10 The maximum range for a projectile occurs when the angle of projection is 45°.

You should look this up yourself. You could try the *Guinness Book of Records*.

Substituting your value for the distance into the equation $u^2 = g \times$ distance will allow you to check your estimation. Remember, however, that this is still just an approximation as the ball did not leave the cricketer's hand at ground level, nor at 45° to the horizontal.

11 Let initial speed of the ball be V.
So $\mathbf{v} = \begin{bmatrix} V \cos 40° \\ V \sin 40° - 10t \end{bmatrix}$

$\mathbf{r} = \begin{bmatrix} Vt \cos 40° \\ Vt \sin 40° - 5t^2 \end{bmatrix}$

so $\begin{bmatrix} Vt \cos 40° \\ Vt \sin 40° - 5t^2 \end{bmatrix} = \begin{bmatrix} 12 \\ 4 \end{bmatrix}$

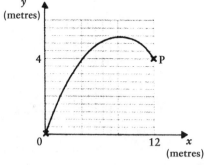

$Vt \cos 40° = 12$

$\Rightarrow t = \dfrac{15.7}{V}$

$Vt \sin 40° - 5t^2 = 4$

Substituting for t, $10.1 - \dfrac{1232}{V^2} = 4$

$\Rightarrow 6.1 V^2 = 1232$

$\Rightarrow V = 14$ m s^{-1}

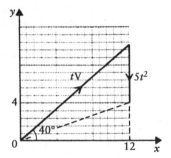

Or using a vector diagram, if the ball is kicked at 40°, then

$5t^2 = 12 \tan 40° - 4 \implies t = 1.10$ seconds

and $V = \dfrac{12}{t \cos 40°} = 14$ m s^{-1}

9   Force and motion

A   Contact forces (p. 96)

Exercise A (p. 99)

1   (a) **A** is the normal contact force;
B is the friction on the sledge;
C is the weight of the sledge.

(b) **D** is the lift force of air on the plane;
E is the drag force of air resistance on the plane;
F is the weight of the plane;
G is the forward thrust of the jet (of air) on the plane due to the jet engines.

(c) **H** is the normal contact force on the toy;
I is its weight;
J is the friction;
K is the push of the child.

(d) **L** is the tension force of the cable on the climber;
M is the weight of the climber;
N is the friction force of the ice face on the climber;
O is the normal contact force of the ice face on the climber.

(e) **P** is the friction force of the bat on the ball;
Q is the weight of the ball;
R is the normal contact force of the bat on the ball.

(f) **S** is the upward lift force on the balloon due to the hot air/cold air density differences;
U is the force of the wind on the balloon;
V is the weight of the balloon.

2

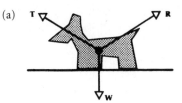

T is the tension in the rope;
F is the friction;
N is the normal contact force;
W is the weight.

3 (a)

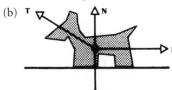

T is the tension in the rope;
R is the contact force;
W is the weight.

(b)

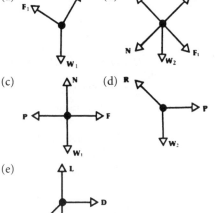

T is the tension in the rope;
N is the normal contact force;
W is the weight;
F is the friction force.

4 (a) (b) (c) (d) (e)

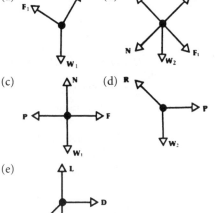

(f)

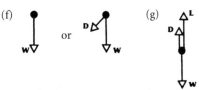

(g)

In the diagrams,

N is the normal contact force;
W is the weight;
P is the push; **R** is contact force;
L is upthrust due to water or air;
D is the force due to air resistance or water resistance;
F is the friction force;
F$_1$ is the friction between girl and toboggan;
F$_2$ is the friction between toboggan and ground;
T is tension.

B Adding forces (p. 100)

1D (a) The tension in each rope is just more than half the weight of the object.

(b) The tension increases.

(c) The tension becomes very large.

The strings can never be horizontal because there would be no upward force to balance *W* downwards.

2 (a) This statement can be validated in the following ways.

(i) Using the rubber band:

The rubber band can be extended to a fixed length by a single newton meter and the force recorded by the newton meter noted. (Remember to zero the newton meter carefully.) The band must then be extended an identical amount using two newton meters and the directions and magnitudes of the two forces can be recorded. The resultant of these two forces can be obtained by drawing, and then compared with the single force needed. It should be noted that an infinite number of pairs of readings can be obtained for the two newton meters. This can be seen clearly from the vector triangle.

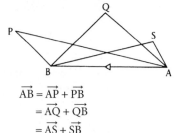

$$\overrightarrow{AB} = \overrightarrow{AP} + \overrightarrow{PB}$$
$$= \overrightarrow{AQ} + \overrightarrow{QB}$$
$$= \overrightarrow{AS} + \overrightarrow{SB}$$

(ii) Using pulleys and masses:

The force needed to support a mass can be measured by a newton meter. An identical force must therefore be produced by the combination of the two strings passing over the pulleys. The tension in each string is equal to the force exerted by the mass suspended by it. Once again the directions and magnitudes of these forces can be noted and a triangle of forces drawn. The pulleys will need to be as frictionless as possible if this experiment is to achieve convincing results.

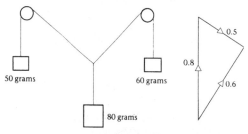

(b) This can be validated in a similar way to (a). In both (i) and (ii) the systems of forces are in equilibrium. Scale drawing of the vectors concerned will show that they combine to give zero. Note that in validating statement (a) with apparatus (i) the forces needed to produce a given extension in an elastic band are equated. In validating (b) the same apparatus is used to show that as the force in the elastic band is equal in magnitude and opposite in direction to the force given on the single newton meter, the three forces (those produced by the elastic band and the two newton meters) will add up to zero.

(c) The magnitudes and directions of the forces exerted by four newton meters attached by strings to a ring can be noted. The hypothesis that they can be added by drawing a vector polygon can be validated by showing that there is a quadrilateral whose sides represent the four forces in both magnitude and direction. Care must be taken with the initialisation of the newton meters when used horizontally.

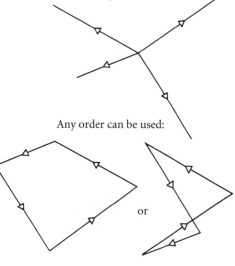

Any order can be used:

or

Exercise B (p. 105)

1 (a) 6.4 N at 39° to the force of 5 N.
   (b) 1.3 N, 88° above the force of 0.8 N.

2 900 N at an angle of 14° to the force of 420 N.

3 113 000 N in the direction of the ship.

4 215 N at an angle of 22° to the vertical.

5 The angle between the forces is 63°.

6 (a) $\mathbf{P} = 4.5$ N at an angle of 117° to the force of 2 N.

   (b) $\mathbf{Q} = 11.7$ N at an angle of 149° to the force of 10 N.

   (c) $\mathbf{F} = 5.4$ N at an angle of 112° to the force of 2 N.

   (d) $\mathbf{T} = 4$ N at an angle of 120° to the force of 4 N.

7 The force required is 98 N.

To estimate the least angle ϕ, first estimate the largest force the two people can apply, say $T = 200$ N.

For $T = 200$, the angle is 22°. In general,

$$\phi = \sin^{-1}\frac{75}{T}.$$

C Resolving forces (p. 106)

Exercise C (p. 107)

1 (a) $\begin{bmatrix} 43.3 \\ 25.0 \end{bmatrix}$

(b) The components are:

49.2 N up the slope;
8.68 N perpendicular to the slope.

(c) The components are:

32.1 N down the slope;
38.3 N perpendicular to the slope.

2 (a)
2.29 N

3.28 N

(b)
6.43 N

7.66 N

(c)

3.5 N

6.06 N

(d)
42.3 N

90.6 N

3 (a) Force diagram

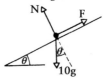
N   F

θ 10g

Equivalent set of forces

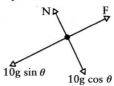
N   F

10g sin θ 10g cos θ

For equilibrium, the resultant force is zero.

i.e. $\begin{bmatrix} N - 10g \cos\theta \\ F - 10g \sin\theta \end{bmatrix} = \begin{bmatrix} 0 \\ 0 \end{bmatrix}$

Thus
$F = 10g \sin\theta = 10g \sin 20° = 33.5$ N

(b) $F = 10g \sin\theta$ newtons and
$N = 10g \cos\theta$ newtons

$\Rightarrow \quad \dfrac{F}{N} = \tan\theta$

4 If you consider directions parallel to and perpendicular to the 11 newton force, then

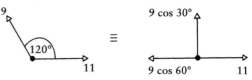

9 cos 30°

$\equiv$

120°   11   9 cos 60°   11

The sum of the forces

$= \begin{bmatrix} 11 - 9\cos 60° \\ 9\cos 30° \end{bmatrix} = \begin{bmatrix} 6.5 \\ 7.79 \end{bmatrix}$

The resultant force is 10.1 newtons at an angle of 50.2° to the 11 newton force.

5 (a) $R = \begin{bmatrix} 2.60 \\ 1.50 \end{bmatrix} + \begin{bmatrix} -1.00 \\ 1.73 \end{bmatrix} + \begin{bmatrix} -1.97 \\ -0.347 \end{bmatrix}$

$= \begin{bmatrix} -0.37 \\ 2.88 \end{bmatrix}$

This has magnitude 2.91 N, making an angle of 82.7° clockwise from the leftward horizontal.

(b) Take the x-axis parallel to the top right 2 N force.

$$\mathbf{R} = \begin{bmatrix} 2 \\ 0 \end{bmatrix} + \begin{bmatrix} -1 \\ 1.73 \end{bmatrix} + \begin{bmatrix} -2 \\ 0 \end{bmatrix} + \begin{bmatrix} 1.29 \\ -1.53 \end{bmatrix}$$

$$= \begin{bmatrix} 0.29 \\ 0.20 \end{bmatrix}$$

This has magnitude 0.35 N and cuts the 120° angle into 35° and 85°, reading anticlockwise.

6   $\mathbf{R} = \begin{bmatrix} 34.6 \\ 20 \end{bmatrix} + \begin{bmatrix} -35 \\ 0 \end{bmatrix} + \begin{bmatrix} 0 \\ -20 \end{bmatrix} = \begin{bmatrix} -0.4 \\ 0 \end{bmatrix}$

It will move in the direction of the 35 N force.

7   Let the tensions be T_1 and T_2, in newtons.

(a) $\begin{bmatrix} T_2 \sin 60° \\ T_2 \cos 60° \end{bmatrix} + \begin{bmatrix} -T_1 \sin 50° \\ T_1 \cos 50° \end{bmatrix} + \begin{bmatrix} 0 \\ -600 \end{bmatrix}$

$= \begin{bmatrix} 0 \\ 0 \end{bmatrix}$

$\Rightarrow T_2 \sin 60° = T_1 \sin 50°$

and $T_2 \cos 60° + T_1 \cos 50° = 600$

$\dfrac{T_1 \sin 50°}{\sin 60°} \times \cos 60° + T_1 \cos 50° = 600$

$\Rightarrow T_1 = 533$ N

and $T_2 = \dfrac{T_1 \sin 50°}{\sin 60°} = 489$ N

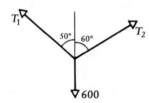

(b) Taking axes parallel and perpendicular to T_2,

$\begin{bmatrix} T_2 \\ 0 \end{bmatrix} + \begin{bmatrix} -T_1 \sin 20° \\ T_1 \cos 20° \end{bmatrix} + \begin{bmatrix} -600 \sin 30° \\ -600 \cos 30° \end{bmatrix}$

$= \begin{bmatrix} 0 \\ 0 \end{bmatrix}$

$\Rightarrow T_2 - T_1 \sin 20° - 600 \sin 30° = 0$

and $T_1 \cos 20° - 600 \cos 30° = 0$

$\Rightarrow T_1 = \dfrac{600 \cos 30°}{\cos 20°} = 553$ N

$T_2 = T_1 \sin 20° + 600 \sin 30°$
$= 489$ N

8   $m = \dfrac{3\sqrt{2}}{100}$ kg = 42 grams

9   Let the tensions in the strings be T_1 and T_2 as shown.

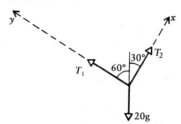

By Newton's second law,

$\begin{bmatrix} T_2 \\ 0 \end{bmatrix} + \begin{bmatrix} 0 \\ T_1 \end{bmatrix} = \begin{bmatrix} 200 \cos 30° \\ 200 \sin 30° \end{bmatrix}$

$T_2 = 100\sqrt{3}$ newtons

$T_1 = 100$ newtons

D   Force and acceleration (p. 109)

1D   A sensible choice of directions in which to resolve would be parallel and perpendicular to the plane. This is because there is no acceleration perpendicular to the plane.

The set of forces is equivalent to:

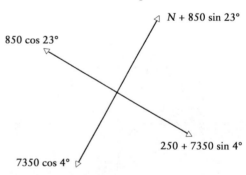

Newton's second law gives:

$\begin{bmatrix} 850 \cos 23° - 250 - 7350 \sin 4° \\ N + 850 \sin 23° - 7350 \cos 4° \end{bmatrix} = m \begin{bmatrix} a \\ 0 \end{bmatrix}$

This gives $N = 7000$ newtons.

The resultant force
$= 850 \cos 23° - 250 - 7350 \sin 4°$
$= 19.719$ or 20 newtons up the plane

The acceleration $a = \dfrac{19.719}{750} = 0.026$ m s^{-2}

up the plane.

Exercise D (p. 111)

1 $N = 11.5$ newtons

The acceleration of the block

$$a = \frac{15 \sin 40° - 2}{1.5}$$

$$a = 5.1 \text{ m s}^{-2}$$

2   The acceleration of the trolley is 0.58 m s^{-2}.

3   The resultant force $\mathbf{R} = 650 - 540 = 110$ N downwards, giving an acceleration of 1.7 m s^{-2}.

If the rope breaks, she will start to accelerate at $g = 10 \text{ m s}^{-2}$.

4   The air resistance is 4 newtons.

5   (a) If the woman is travelling with constant speed she is in equilibrium so the contact force between her and the lift is 600 newtons.

   (b) If she moves upward with acceleration 1.5 m s^{-2} then, if the normal contact force is R,

$$R - 600 = 60 \times 1.5$$

$$R = 690 \text{ newtons}$$

   (c) If she moves downward with acceleration 1.5 m s^{-2} then, if the normal contact force is R,

$$600 - R = 60 \times 1.5$$

$$R = 510 \text{ newtons}$$

E   Model of static friction (p. 111)

1D

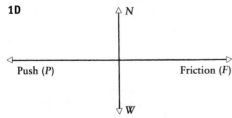

When no one pushes the crate there is no friction force. As P increases, F increases in order to maintain equilibrium. At any time, $P = F$.

When the fifth person helps, the crate accelerates from rest and $P > F$. So there seems to be a maximum possible value for F.

The magnitude of the friction force therefore equals the magnitude of P, until F reaches its maximum value.

The maximum value of F is likely to depend upon such things as

● the types of material in contact

● the weight of the crate

● the area of contact.

Exercise E (p. 113)

1   (a) Let F be the friction force and N the normal contact force. The crate is in equilibrium, so by Newton's second law,

$$F = 100 \sin 30° = 50 \text{ newtons}$$

and

$$N = 100 \cos 30° = 87 \text{ newtons}$$

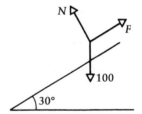

   (b) But the crate is about to slip, so $F = \mu N$.

$$\Rightarrow \quad 50 = 86.6\mu$$

$$\Rightarrow \quad \mu = 0.58$$

2   The rubber is on the point of slipping so $F = 0.7N$. But by Newton's second law, along and perpendicular to the slope,

$$F = mg \sin \alpha \text{ and } N = mg \cos \alpha$$

so $\tan \alpha = 0.7$

$$\alpha = 35°$$

The table can be tilted to 35°.

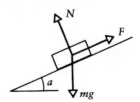

3 (a) The greatest angle of slope is 50°.
    (b) The friction force is 500 newtons.

4 (a) $T = 840$ N
    (b) $T = 880$ N

5 The climber is in equilibrium, so $F \leqslant \mu N$.

$N = 1000 \cos 80° = 173.6$ newtons

and $T + F = 1000 \sin 80° = 984.8$ newtons

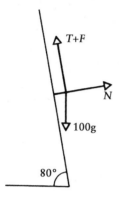

Now $F \leqslant 0.9N = 156.2$

but F can act either up or down the slope depending on which way the body is trying to move, so

$1141 \geqslant T \geqslant 828.6$

The tension in the rope lies approximately between 830 newtons and 1140 newtons.

F Models of sliding friction (p. 113)

1 A suitable value for u in the first 20 metres is the average speed $\dfrac{20}{11.9} = 1.68$ m s^{-1}.

2 (a) For the first few seconds, the standard model $F = 0$ provides a reasonable fit to the experimental data and is therefore satisfactory.

    (b) For $t > 10$ seconds, the model is not satisfactory and must be modified.

3 (a) Using a graphic calculator a curve can be fitted to the data. A reasonable fit is obtained by using the curve $x = 2.05t - 0.03t^2$. Hence a value of 0.06 for $\dfrac{F}{m}$ would appear to give a good model.

    (b) Constant resistive force seems to be a good model. It is interesting to note that the estimated initial speed of the stone is greater in this model than in the simple model.

Exercise F (p. 117)

1 Let μ be the coefficient of sliding friction between the block and table.

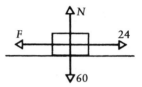

The block is in equilibrium, so by Newton's second law

$F = 24$ and $N = 60$

But the block is sliding so $F = \mu N$

$\Rightarrow \quad 24 = 60\mu$

$\quad\quad \mu = 0.4$

2 The puck is sliding freely so $F = 0.02N$

$\Rightarrow \quad F = 0.02$

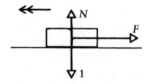

By Newton's second law, $\quad -F = ma$

$\Rightarrow \quad -0.02 = 0.1a$

$\quad\quad a = -0.2$

The initial speed is 10 m s^{-1}

so $v = 10 - 0.2t \quad\quad t = 20$

$v = 6$ m s^{-1} after 20 seconds.

3 $F = 0.3N = 3$ newtons, but by Newton's second law,

$0 - F = ma \quad a = -3$

Initial speed is 5 m s^{-1}, so $v = 5 - 3t$ and when $v = 0$, $t = \frac{5}{3}$

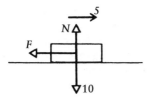

Now $s = ut + \frac{1}{2}at^2$

$\qquad = 5 \times \frac{5}{3} + \frac{1}{2} \times -3 \times \frac{25}{9}$

$\qquad = \frac{25}{6}$ metres

4   The normal contact force N

$\qquad = 5g - 60 \sin 40°$

$\qquad = 11.4$ newtons

$F = \mu N = 6.86$ newtons

The net forward force $= 60 \cos 40° - 6.86$

$\qquad\qquad\qquad\qquad = 39.1$ newtons

So the accceleration is $\dfrac{39.1}{5} = 7.8$ m s^{-2}

5E If the particle is sliding down the slope, F acts up the slope.

$P + F = mg \sin \phi$ and $N = mg \cos \phi$ by Newton's second law,

but $F = \mu N$

so $P + \mu mg \cos \phi = mg \sin \phi$

$P = mg (\sin \phi - \mu \cos \phi)$

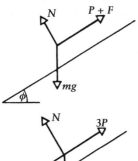

If the particle is sliding up the slope at constant speed, F acts down the plane,

so $3P - F = mg \sin \phi$ and $N = mg \cos \phi$

$\Rightarrow 3P = mg (\sin \phi + \mu \cos \phi)$

but $P = mg (\sin \phi - \mu \cos \phi)$

$\Rightarrow 3(\sin \phi - \mu \cos \phi) = \sin \phi + \mu \cos \phi$

$\Rightarrow 2 \sin \phi = 4\mu \cos \phi$

$\Rightarrow \tan \phi = 2\mu$

10   Connected bodies

A   Static two-body problems (p. 119)

1D   (a)

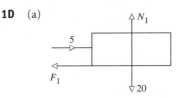

$N_1 = 20, F_1 = 5$

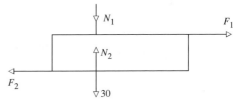

$N_2 = 50, F_2 = 5$

(b)   Maximum friction force between book and block $= 0.4 \times 20 = 8$ N. Maximum friction force between block and table $= 0.2 \times 50 = 10$ N.

Slipping will take place first between the book and the block – as soon as the push exceeds 8 N.

2D   (c)   There are internal forces within the bicycle chain, at the hubs and indeed at all parts of the machine. The external forces are provided by the boy and girl, and also by the ground on the tyres. The horizontal forces are on the pedal in a backwards direction and consequent friction on the back wheel which is in a forwards direction. The force on the pedal is the larger one so the bicycle moves backwards. This surprisingly causes the pedal to rotate anticlockwise (looking at the picture in Chapter 1), but relative to the ground the girl's hand nevertheless moves in the same direction as the bicycle does.

(d) It is helpful to consider the forces on you and the broom together. Then the force between you and the broom is an internal force. The external forces are the weight and the upward forces on the feet and the broom. When the broom presses down on the scales, they register the full weight. When the floor provides much of the upthrust, the scales give a reduced reading.

Exercise A (p. 121)

1   20 N and 50 N, assuming the strings have negligible weight.

2    $P = 0.3 \times 40 + 0.7 \times 60 = 54$

The required force is 54 N, and the normal contact force is then 42 N.

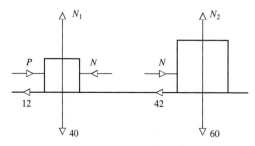

3   12 N

4    $F_1 = 20 \sin 10° = 3.5$,
     $F_2 = 50 \sin 10° = 8.7$
     $N_1 = 20 \cos 10°$, $N_2 = 50 \cos 10°$
     $\dfrac{F_1}{N_1} \leqslant \mu_1 \Rightarrow \mu_1 \geqslant \tan 10° = 0.18$;
     $\mu_2 \geqslant 0.18$ similarly.

5   (a) So that you will accelerate at the same rate as the car, there must be a substantial forward force on you. This will be largely provided by pressure on your back from the seat. The corresponding backwards force on the car means that marginally more fuel is used than if you were not in the car.

(b) The main force will usually be on your feet. If this is not sufficient and/or you do not brace your body, it may be necessary to provide an extra backwards force by pressing your hand against the front seat or dashboard.

B   Connected bodies in motion (p. 122)

1   (a) $P - 70g = 70 \times 2 \Rightarrow P = 840$ N
     (b) $T - 500g - P = 500 \times 2 \Rightarrow T = 6840$ N.
          Also $T - 570g = 570 \times 2 \Rightarrow T = 6840$ N
     (c) (i) $P =$ man's weight
          (ii) $P <$ man's weight
          (iii) During the descent, P is less than the man's weight when the lift speeds up, and more than his weight when it slows down.

Exercise B (p. 123)

1    $a = 1.5$ m s^{-2};   thrust $= 144a = 216$ N

2   (a) $a = \frac{1}{2}$, $P = 1650$
     (b) $a = \frac{10}{13}$, $P = 2540$

3 For the load, $T + 30 - 400 = 40 \times 6$,

$T = 610$ N.

For the load + parachute,

$U + 30 - 420 = 42 \times 6$, $U = 642$ N.

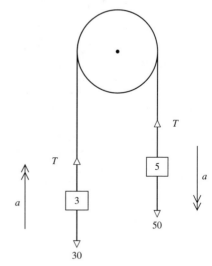

4 Upthrust = 8900 N; initial normal reaction on man = 900 N

Later, $8900 - 8400 = 840a$, $a = 0.595$ and $N - 900 = 90 \times 0.595$, $N = 954$

$v = -8 + 30 \times 0.595 = 9.85$

The normal contact force is 950 N and the speed after 30 seconds is 9.9 m s^{-1} (upwards).

5 The acceleration is $\dfrac{1000}{1200}$ m s^{-2}, the normal reaction is 2170 N and the distance is 9.6 m.

6 $\left.\begin{array}{l} 50 - T = 5a \\ T - 30 = 3a \end{array}\right\}$ give $a = \dfrac{20}{8} = 2.5$,

$$T = 37.5$$

The acceleration is 2.5 m s^{-2} and the tension in the string is 37.5 N.

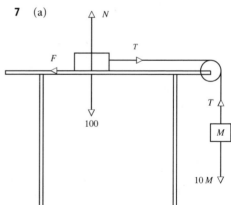

7 (a)

$N = 100$, $F \leqslant 30$

(b) (i) When $M = 2$, there will be no motion and $F = T = 20$.

   (ii) When $M = 4$, there will be an acceleration and $F = 30$.

      $40 - T = 4a$ and $T - 30 = 10a$.

      The tension is 37 N.